TAKING
A YEAR OFF

by
VAL BUTCHER

with additional material
by
Lynne Budden

TROTMAN

This edition published in 1993 in Great Britain by
Trotman and Company Limited
12 Hill Rise, Richmond, Surrey TW10 6UA

© Trotman and Company Limited

ISBN 0 85660 206 X

Typeset by Type Study, Scarborough

Reproduced, printed and bound in Great Britain

Contents

Contents

Taking a year off: Route finding

Thinking about taking a year off?
How can you use this book to help?

Don't just read from front to back – you can use it *in any order* depending on how far your plans have gone.

If you are planning to take time out between school and further study, or after higher education, you will find many reference books which will give you the information you need.

see 'BOOKCASE' **140**

If you don't know where to start, jog your memory about what is available.

see 'WHAT EXACTLY CAN I DO?' *for virgins* **23**

. . . and you can remind yourself about essential things to check out.

see 'CHECKLISTS' **133**

You may talk to a number of people who have already had time out, and pick up useful hints from their experiences.

if not, 'THE BEST LAID PLANS . . .' will help **65**

. . . and you will need to weigh up all the general issues. Read what groups of sixth formers, undergraduates and graduates felt were the main issues.

see 'WHEN TO DO IT'   **7**

BUT – There is a lot more to making good plans than all this! It is a very personal decision and you owe it to yourself to work out how a year off would work for you.

What are other people going to think about you taking a year off? Read how some families, future employers and college staff feel, and think about how this may affect you.

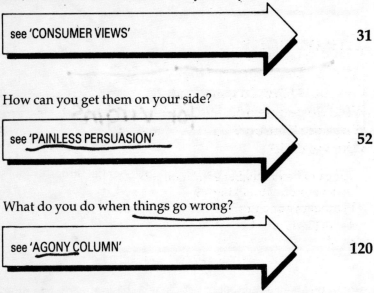

see 'CONSUMER VIEWS'   **31**

How can you get them on your side?

see 'PAINLESS PERSUASION'   **52**

What do you do when things go wrong?

see 'AGONY COLUMN'   **120**

FINALLY – Is it really for *you*? Work out for yourself how a year off might fit into *your* life.

see 'IS IT FOR ME?'   **128**

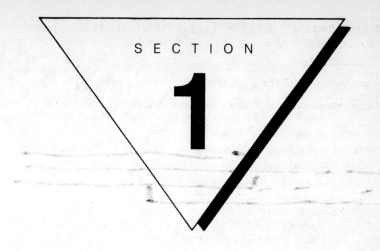

S E C T I O N

1.

The options

Time out? How do you decide?

Getting off the treadmill, taking time out from study or from work may prove to be a good idea at any time of life. If your chances of getting a job are slim until next year's recruitment, there are positive ways in which you can spend your time. And then getting away from it all, and reflecting on where you are going, can feel great. Add to that the experience of going to new places and meeting different people and you can begin to feel quite positive about it. All you need to avoid is the temptation to drift aimlessly through six, 12 or even 18 months – one thing you can be absolutely certain of is that when you rejoin the education system, or take up employment, *someone, somewhere is going to want to know what you did with your time, and why you did it.*

So, what can you do, why might you be considering it, and when would be the best time to do it? Take a brief look at some of the key issues before exploring the options in depth.

What do people do?

Anything, or nothing at all, but with a little research and planning the possibilities may prove endless. Below are just a few examples of activities that people have got involved in:

- **working on a kibbutz**
- **voluntary work in India**
- **au pair**
- **waiter/waitress**
- **bar worker**
- **agricultural labourer**
- **grape picking, and travelling in France**
- **conservation volunteer**
- **temporary secretarial work**
- **employment in catering in Australia**
- **full-time work in the UK**

- **voluntary work camps**
- **work in a ski resort (chambermaid)**
- **language assistant in schools abroad**

And so on

Why take time out?

Your decision to take time out may well meet with some criticism, so it always helps to be fairly sure of your motives and to be aware of some of the difficulties you might encounter along the way.

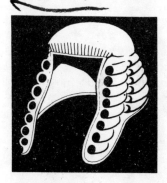

Here are some quotes taken from people who felt they benefited from taking time out:

The case for:

- **it's a break from the education system**
- **you get time to rethink your options**
- **you can improve your CV by showing that you have made good use of a time of unemployment**
- **you can go abroad to learn a language**
- **you get to see the culture and lifestyles of another country from the inside**
- **some colleges like you to have taken time out first**
- **you get cheap travel with InterRail**
- **you broaden your horizons**

- you get time to decide on your course and whether you really want to do it
- you meet lots of different kinds of people
- you learn to fend for yourself
- you can get rid of exam pressures for a while
- you can earn some money to supplement the grant
- you get more confidence
- doing community work makes you feel you have given something back
- you can travel – you can't do it so easily when you're working or at college

Here are some more quotes from people who felt they had reservations about the usefulness of a year out:

The case against:

- your friends get a year ahead of you at university
- it was hard to get back into academic study
- some college departments don't like you deferring entry
- when I returned to the UK, I found I had missed the closing-date for application to some companies
- I hoped that a year out would help me decide my career plans, but I still didn't know what I wanted to do when I got back
- it was hard to give up the money and go back to living on a grant

- it was difficult to decide whether to give up the job I'd got, as I could have got on in it
- it was easy to lose touch with friends who'd gone to college earlier
- my family weren't keen on the idea
- employers didn't seem impressed with my year out when I went for interviews

When to do it?

For many people the chance to take time out for a few months at a time comes between A-level/H grades and higher education. Some delay the break until they've finished a higher diploma or degree course and take a year or more out before going into a job. A-level students and graduates seeking employment sometimes find this takes longer than they expected, and want to use the time creatively.

You can also have time out which is built into a sandwich course (a period of work experience related to what you are studying), or your university or company might arrange foreign exchanges. Some people take time out after having worked full-time for a number of years.

Time out before higher education

Why take time out now?

- fed up with studying, getting stale, need a break
- take up a job, earn money, helps with grant
- get experience related to later choice of career
- spend a year abroad to develop language fluency
- spend some time away from home before going to university
- time to decide on course of higher education, or even if higher education is what you want at all

7

Why not to take time out now?

- **want to get study out of the way in one go**
- **planning a sandwich course, so time out comes later**
- **college department may prefer you to start immediately**

(SEE Becky's story on page 77, Rose's on page 66 and Janet's on page 92.)

A-level students talking

A group of sixth form students: Ann, Ian, Janine, Cathy, Sarah and Colin, discuss their plans with a careers tutor. They are considering whether to take a year off after A-levels, and before going on to a course of higher education.

Q – Why do you want to take a year out?

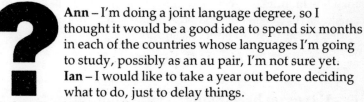

Ann – I'm doing a joint language degree, so I thought it would be a good idea to spend six months in each of the countries whose languages I'm going to study, possibly as an au pair, I'm not sure yet.
Ian – I would like to take a year out before deciding what to do, just to delay things.
Cathy – I've had two offers from people that I know to au pair, in London and in France, and as I want to do teacher training I think it would be good experience to be with kids for a while, to see how I get on with them!
Sarah – I'm buying time, I want to take a break from education, to get out of the system for a while. After all I've been in it since I was five!
Colin – I want to do some voluntary work before doing a degree; I think it will help my later career. I'm aiming to be a social worker.

Q – Where did the idea of taking a year out come from?

Ian – I was talking to a cousin of mine who had taken time out to go to America for a year; it sounded OK.
Janine – I want to do speech therapy, so I thought it would be a good idea to do some voluntary work with people to help my career prospects later.
Sarah – It was my idea entirely, I just want a break from study and exams.

Q – What exactly do you want to do?

Sarah – I want to travel. I'm thinking of working on a kibbutz next year.

Ian – I want to do Camp America for a while and then spend some time travelling.

Ann – I might like to work in the UK for about six months in an ordinary job so that I can save some money. If I can get a job that is! Then I will go abroad, perhaps as an au pair.

Cathy – I've got a few ideas. First I want to work for a few months. I know someone who will definitely take me on here for a few months, so I can save some money. Then I'm going to Australia (I've been before) to travel and stay with people I know. I've also got an offer of a summer job in Switzerland next year.

Q – Have you been in touch with your future colleges to find out what their reactions are to students taking a year off?

Cathy – I found something in one of the alternative prospectuses that said they encouraged students to take a year out.

Colin – Someone I know said that they don't like you taking a year off as they want to get their courses filled up.

Ann – I've contacted the department head who said he thought it would be a good idea if I deferred entry – as long as I did something 'relevant' to my course and didn't just bum around!

Q – What plans have you made so far?

Colin – I've written to the department heads to ask what they think of deferring entry. I've read some of the alternative prospectuses, like Cathy, but they don't tell you what the colleges' attitudes are – it seems to depend on department heads.

Ann – I'm applying already, but for deferred entry, so that I know I've got a place to come back to. I don't want to have to come home for an interview once I'm away. I've written to some schools abroad, to ask them if I can work as a junior assistant with them. I feel that I have to get things fixed up as soon as possible, because it is so difficult to get a temporary job here.

Cathy – I've got a list of agencies that organize au pair work and I'm going to write to them.

Sarah – I want to get a job locally. I've asked the Careers Office to keep my name down for vacancies, but I realize that it will be quite difficult to find anything. I have a Saturday job which pays quite well, and I think I'll be offered some part time work there from October.

Q – What do your parents think of your ideas?

Sarah – My mother isn't keen at all; she thinks I'm just going to waste a year, though I want to get a job. I don't think I'll be wasting my time, but maybe she's afraid that I'll get depressed if I can't get a job. I think she's anxious because I don't really know what I want to do yet.

Ann – My parents are quite keen now they know what I want to do. They weren't keen at first, but they think I'll get some experience if I can get a job abroad for a year before doing my language course.

Janine – Mine were very much against it; they couldn't see that getting some work experience would help my career later on.

Q – How are you going to support yourself financially?

Ian – I've been saving up so that I'll have enough money to travel after I've done some voluntary work.

Colin – I'm going to do voluntary work. They say they will provide board and lodging and little pocket money, so I think I'll get by, even if I'm not rich. And anyway it'll get me used to being poor when I'm a student!

Ann – My parents say they will give me some help if I need it, as long as I don't waste my time.

Sarah – A friend of mine made a claim as soon as she finished at school, and got income support. I'll do that if I'm not fixed up by the time I leave.

Q – What problems do you think you may encounter?

Sarah – Just getting a job; there are just so few vacancies. And if I go for a permanent job, I'm not sure that I'll be happy to say that I want to make a career of it, knowing I have a college place for next year.

Colin – I'm not sure whether all colleges approve of you taking a year out. Mostly they seem to think it's OK if you do something they think is relevant. But if I do a lot of travelling – or my plans fall through – they might think I've been messing about.

Cathy – It might be a bit difficult to get used to studying again after a year.

Ann – I want to be an au pair, but it's difficult to be sure that you are going to get a good place to go – they might make you do the washing up all the time!

Planning your entry

For many people, taking time out before higher education is an obvious and attractive option. In the normal course of events, an A level or BTEC National student would apply for a place during their final year at school or college but defer entry for some twenty months.

But changes in the way that applications are administered are being debated. And if any of those changes were to go ahead then you would have to think differently about your time off, and make different plans.

Taking a Year Off *asked* **Tony Higgins**, *Chief Executive of the Polytechnics Central Admissions System, (to be superseded by the Universities and Colleges Admissions Service) for his views on what the future held for higher education admissions:*

Tony Higgins – The first thing to say is that entry to higher education is bound to change enormously over the next ten years. The typical entrant will no longer be a full time student offering high grades at A-level. Because grants are lower in value, and state benefits not so readily available, more students are likely to study part-time rather than full-time, or live at home.

Others will move in and out of higher education as they earn the money to pay for their studies. Mature entrants will be able to use their work experience to get credit for entry to courses, at different levels.

And the qualifications offered by school leavers will be different too: only a fifth of the young people that the Government anticipates entering higher education in the year 2000 will have A-levels!

Taking a Year Off – Are the universities making changes then?

13

Tony Higgins – Yes, certainly. They are making courses more accessible by offering entry to people with work experience, under the Credit Accumulation and Transfer Scheme. And grappling with the problems of offering places to students who do not have predicted grades in traditional qualifications like A-levels. Some of the students who follow a GNVQ or modular A-level course, for example, may not decide how those courses will be accredited until well after they have applied for higher education!

And now the higher education institutions are discussing radical changes to the terms or semesters of the academic year, which will affect admissions procedures.

Taking a Year Off – What will this mean for the current UCCA/PCAS applications procedures?

Tony Higgins – A central clearing house system will continue, as the most efficient way of dealing with the needs of students and institutions.

But there are many reasons why the procedures should change. At the moment school leavers are having to commit themselves to a course of study at a time when their ideas and interests are changing rapidly. And because of the length of time between courses being listed and actually starting – some twenty months – students are often unaware of the up-to-date range of courses on offer.

Elements of the current system rely too heavily on assumptions of the 1960s, when the numbers of applicants and institutions were smaller. And the universities are constrained in their admissions policies by the timing of government allocation of funds; sometimes they do not know how many students can be accepted for a course until well into the interview and selection programme. So early applicants may have an advantage because tutors are keen to make most of their offers well ahead of closing dates. But if the number of places for a particular course increases during the selection period, students applying later may be given lower targets to achieve.

14

Taking a Year Off – Is there a fair solution?

Tony Higgins – There is a strong argument for processing all applications after the examination results are known. Then all the applicants would be judged against the examination performance needed for entry. Students would be more mature – and more certain in their own minds of what they wanted to do. And the list of available courses would be up to date.

A more ordered application process would be cheaper to manage, and more streamlined. And it would be possible to build in the new developments in assessment, such as the Records of Achievement that increasing numbers of school leavers will be producing.

There is clearly no opportunity to do this within the current timetable, but the restructuring of the HE academic year might enable students to start courses in November or December, even January; or enter at two points in the year. Another alternative that has been discussed is a four term school year.

The students entering higher education in the 1990s will present different challenges to the admissions process. So it will have to respond, to change.

Clearly, any such changes would have some effect on your strategy, when it comes to taking time off. You may be able to choose to use a shorter length of time to work or travel, while still going to university with your peers. Or you might choose to stagger your entry for a period of time other than the traditional academic year. Part time study may become a feature of time in work that would otherwise have been considered 'time out'. And the number of students obtaining deferred places may be greatly reduced.

Taking time out after a degree

Why take time out now? – The case for:

- you've earned it after all those years of study
- you feel like a break before entering a career
- you need time to wind down from exams
- you can't get a job in this year's recruitment cycle and want to enhance your CV
- it's the only time when you can travel or do voluntary work before settling into a job
- if you don't do it now you may *never* do it
- finals are tough, and applying for jobs now can mean too much pressure
- time out now can give you time to concentrate on applying for jobs later on

Why not to take time out now – The case against:

- when you apply for a job later on, your CV could have gaps on it unless you take care filling it in
- employers may not be impressed with your choice of activity during your time out
- you may take a few months out and find you've missed various employers' recruiting dates, and have to wait for the next round of recruitment next year
- if you go abroad you may not be available when interviews take place for jobs next year

(SEE Jackie's story on page 71, Finlay's on page 85 and Daniel's on page 104.)

Undergraduates talking

Sally, Mark and Claire, three undergraduates, share their experiences of taking time out (or not, as the case may be), between A-levels and their degree courses. And they look ahead at the pros and cons of taking another break – between graduating and taking permanent jobs.

Q – What did you do after your A-level year?

?

Sally – I took a year out, much to my parents' surprise! I suppose I sprang it on them, and didn't really plan what I was going to do with the year. But I felt quite strongly that I wanted some space for myself before starting another course. In some ways they were right – I took a nannying job at short notice, but didn't get on with the family, and ended up being unemployed for about ten months.

Mark – I went on to a foundation course in Theatre Studies after school, which included a lot of practical work. I took part in lots of college productions and directed one play, which was very good experience. And the head of department was excellent – he arranged theatre placements, so I could feel I was gaining experience in the 'real world' of theatre, too.

Claire – I went straight on from school to university, like most of my friends. I suppose we believed that universities wouldn't want you if you took a year off. And maybe that you'd find it difficult to get back into the habit of studying. And all the time we were getting messages about the poor job situation. From where we sat, it seemed only logical to go straight on to college.

Q – What did you gain?

Sally – Despite the fact that things didn't work out as expected, I learned an awful lot about myself, about where I wanted to go, and about being independent. In some respects it sort of 'knocked school out of me'. Even though I didn't do anything definite, I was still very glad that I didn't go straight on to university.

Mark – Yes that's how I felt. In some senses I suppose I had a 'protected year out' – my time was structured, and I had a strong sense of direction. But I had all the fun of doing largely what I wanted to do.

Claire – I have mixed feelings about going straight on from school to university. Some of the people I know who took time out do seem to have a clearer idea of where they are going after their degree. But there are one or two who haven't benefited – they are just several years older than I am, with experience of very routine jobs. And now they're wondering if they will stand a chance in the graduate job market, because of their age. On balance I am happy that I started my course when I did.

Q – What do you think about a year out after graduation?

Sally – I'm going for it! This time it will be much easier to take the decision without feeling that I'm letting someone down. Even though my parents still have the same view as when I left school, I shall be older, and more relaxed about making a go of it. I want to take another full-time course after my degree, a TEFL (Teaching English as a Foreign Language) course. But for that I need some teaching experience. So I don't know if you would say that I am taking time out, or whether I am starting on my 'career'. This time I shall make sure that what I do in the year between finishing one course and starting the next is 'relevant'.

Claire – I think people are more willing to accept that you are going to take a year out after a degree – because you have got a qualification behind you. Sally knows what she is going to do. I am not so sure about things, so a year out for me will be a break from studying, to help me work out where I'm going.

Mark – I'm still thinking about it. My aim is to get into theatre directing – somehow! I may take an indefinite period of time out in order to push forward with this. But I'm also contemplating doing an MA, and have some ideas of where I could go after that. Maybe I'll devote myself to the theatre for a year or two and if at the end of that time I haven't achieved what I want, I'll reconsider.

Q – What do you think future employers will think about taking time out after graduation?

Claire – I think some employers might think that you'd messed around for a year and not done anything productive. Once I've decided what I want to do, I will have to convince future employers that my time out has helped me make sure that the job I take is a firm choice, that I'll have some commitment to it.
Mark – I see it as a positive advantage to have experience after a degree. No theatre company is going to look at me if I cannot actually say "I'm not fresh from college, I'm not green and naive, I do know what I'm on about". It will be the most beneficial thing I could have.
Sally – Yes, but that wouldn't work for all types of employers, would it? The milk round recruiters will be less likely to consider you after a year out because they have a completely new supply of graduates coming out each July.
Claire – The job market makes it worse. I'm not ready to commit myself to a 'milk round' type training scheme. So I shall have to spend time this year working out how I am going to fill next year. And thinking how and when I can get back into the graduate job market. Apparently I can use the university careers service near to my home, so I will be able to get access to reference material, on employers. And I shall line up a vocational course, something like secretarial training, as an insurance policy.

Q – What problems might you encounter?

Mark – Money! It has to be the biggest problem. You have to find a way of supporting yourself. And probably a way of paying back your loan at the same time. The worst scenario would be to have to live at home, broke, with your parents getting neurotic.
Claire – And the job situation is pretty desperate. Even the very

routine jobs are difficult to come by – and very badly paid. Once I'm living back at home it will be hard work to keep in touch with the graduate job market, things like closing dates for applications, and knowing which employers recruit all year and so on. I suppose I'll have more time to write letters and approach employers direct – but I'm not looking forward to organizing all that.

Sally – One of my problems is that my boyfriend lives in my home town. He thought I'd do four years at college and then be home, but now I'm taking another year out and then going back into education for another year. He thinks it's going to be never-ending. I can't see where I'll end up yet.

Q – If you had to choose, when would you take time out?

Mark – Between school and degree, most definitely, because that is the period of your life during which you mature, and you are a much better person for doing it then.

Sally – Yes, I would agree. Looking around, the mature students have a much stronger and more definite approach to their work, and produce better work for it. You have to be strong to come back to study if you've been out too long, but I think you bring so much more with you.

Mark – Also, if you take the break after your degree you have to be sure that you can make a very good job of selling that decision – saying what you've gained, skills and so on. Otherwise you are worse off in the job market. If you take a year off after A-levels, you have less to lose.

Claire – Maybe it's a question of when *you* need to take the time out.

Sally – Claire's right. You have to do what is right for you, rather than go along with other people's ideas for your future. In the end, it's *your* decision, it's *your* life.

A year out on a sandwich course

Why take time out this way?

- you can choose various options like thick or thin sandwich courses, giving more or less time out in work
- the sandwich option is available mainly in language, engineering, science, teaching and business studies courses
- you don't have to explain it because it's part of the course
- colleges often find placements for you
- you can earn some money half-way through a course
- you can get experience relevant to your course and choice of job
- you're not alone, your friends on the course are doing the same thing
- you get an automatic break from study
- you may gain skills not directly relevant to your course, such as team working

Why decide against taking time out this way?

- it can make the course seem harder
- it may be harder to get back into study after a year out
- you might get a bad placement that puts you off your original choice of career (maybe not a bad thing if you find that out now)
- you may have to find your own placements before and during a course
- you may have to find your own job or accommodation at home or abroad

(SEE also Julian's experiences on page 101.)

Time out from work

Why wait until now?

- you may never have had the time or money to spare before
- you may feel you are overdue for a break, having worked with only a couple of weeks' break at any time in a year
- you may have taken a wrong turn and need time to reflect on career decisions
- it could be a chance to retrain for something else
- courses with financial assistance could be available
- it could be an opportunity to do voluntary work
- 'a change is as good as a rest'
- it may be time to broaden your horizons and see something of the world

Why decide not to take time out from employment?

- your employer is unlikely to share your views on the benefits of taking time out
- you could be giving up long service perks such as longer holidays and seniority
- you may find difficulty in getting back into employment on your return
- it's more risky than at any other time, you could lose your sense of security
- your job record may suffer when you re-apply – unless you can present your time out as a positive experience

(SEE also Ravinder's story on page 109 and Anila's on page 81.)

What exactly can I do?

The various alternatives for taking time out
are briefly looked at here, and discussed
in more detail in the following chapter.
These options have been
grouped into the following
broad areas:

- **working abroad**
- **travel, holidays, courses abroad**
- **voluntary work, at home or abroad**
- **full-time regular employment in the UK**
- **short courses in the UK**
- **'a mixture'**

Nobody is going to find the perfect solution to every option. To
help you decide, here are some ideas for The Case For, and The
Case Against . . .

1. Working abroad

On the face of it a job abroad for a year sounds pretty glamorous, but if regular employment is what you are after, then a good deal of planning ahead needs to be done. Voluntary work, or working holidays, may be easier to plan than working abroad if you've no experience and no languages, and are dealt with later. What can be said in favour or against working abroad?

For:
- your future career may offer no chance of working abroad, so taking time out might give you your only opportunity to live and work abroad for a time
- you could find the time to travel around your host country
- you can see another country and its culture from close quarters – and that's different from being on holiday
- it can provide an opportunity to learn or brush up on language skills
- you can obtain some types of work without already having the language, or go to an English-speaking country
- you gain experience in a type of work different to that which you are considering for a career
- you may 'broaden your horizons' and outlook generally
- you can get used to being a 'worker' before going back to being a student, if that is your plan
- you get a (hopefully!) refreshing break, whether from education or work

But it can't all be good, so what are the negatives?

Against:
- it could cost you – fares to and from the country, as well as travelling around within it
- you could get homesick
- you might miss your friends and the social life you have at home

- it can be lonely until you meet people and sort out a new social life
- it could turn out to be all work and little play
- at worst you might feel you are being exploited, and have no rights as a new employee
- you could get out of the habit of studying and find it hard to resume if you are going back into education
- you could get restless and find it hard to settle down again
- it isn't easy to organize a full-time rewarding job abroad

2. Travel, holidays, courses abroad

An even more glamorous sounding option – travel and holidays, or possibly attending courses abroad. The spirit of adventure let loose for a while, the absence of responsibility for anyone but yourself, the freedom to disappear off into the wide blue yonder. . . . Again, the news can't be all good, so what should be taken into account?

For:
- you can see an awful lot of the world in six months or a year
- it may be the only time you allow yourself to indulge in so much time for travelling or holidays, and it'll be different from two weeks in Benidorm
- you can afford the time to stop and experience places of interest
- a language course abroad can give you the time and inspiration to really get to grips with the language as it is used
- 'funny things' happen abroad, which you will inevitably put down to experience, which should help you to mature and cope with life better – at least that's what they say!

Against:
- it's going to cost you, even if you can get student discounts

25

- taking courses abroad may be expensive, though a part-time job can help
- on a future CV a year of self-indulgent travel could look frivolous if not explained fully
- you could encounter any number of difficult situations, which would require you to 'think on your feet'
- if you don't have a travelling companion you could get sick of your own company
- with bad luck you could have money or documents stolen and jams like that are harder to cope with away from home

3. Voluntary work

Voluntary work is seldom totally voluntary. In other words, many organizations that take you on will provide free board and lodging, and an amount of pocket money, which in some cases can be quite generous. Many types of work are available, in your own home town, elsewhere in the UK, and in many foreign countries. So, what's in it for you?

For:
- it's your chance to give something back to society
- whatever you do you are likely to feel that it is worthwhile, necessary and of benefit to others
- you may be able to gain work experience that will be relevant to your future career
- you gain experience of work generally, the nine-to-five routine if you haven't tried it before
- you are likely to get a chance to travel at some point during your time out
- you are likely to meet a lot of people, and in many cases will have 'colleagues', so it's less likely you'll be lonely

Against:
- while you will have money to live on, it won't be much

- if you've little money, you'll have to use your savings to travel on
- you may be asked in advance to commit yourself to serving for a set period of time

4. Employment

Taking a year out from study in order to take up regular paid employment is possible straight after A-levels, or during a course of higher education – though usually only as part of a sandwich course. In many parts of the country, the employment situation doesn't make it an easy option, though with planning and forethought it's still a possibility.

For:
- you can earn some money, use it for holidays or to supplement the grant
- you can take a break from education to see how the 'nine-to-fivers' live
- it's a way of getting out of the educational system for a while to give yourself the chance to decide whether you really want to continue studying, or take up a career now
- you can check out a line of work before committing yourself to choosing a higher education course
- you can gain experience that will help your practical understanding of a subject you wish to study later on
- future employers may find that your experience of work has made you a more practical person and less 'idealistic' than they think some students are
- you can have all the benefits of normal employees, like paid holidays, sick leave etc.
- you may find your sense of responsibility and maturity are helped by working
- you can be financially independent, live away from home if you prefer

27

- you may make contacts with employers who might remember you later, when you are ready to take up a career permanently
- you can 'hedge your bets' for a year, and if you decide against higher education, then you've a foot in the door already when it comes to employment

Against:
- you end up a year behind your friends who went off to university before you
- the experience you gain may not be relevant to your future career
- the job situation may make if difficult for you to find a job you like
- you may be earning money, but you'll be expected to pay for your keep, and for lodgings if away from home
- work can mess up your social life, if you have to get up early in the mornings and your student friends are late risers
- you may suffer from a general feeling of loss of freedom, being tied to working hours
- you can get used to earning decent money, which is hard to give up to live on a grant
- you may find it impossible to get a job, and feel that you are wasting valuable time

5. Short courses in the UK

There are many skills which can be useful to you throughout life, some of which you may not be able to pick up while you are on a course of higher education, or while you are in permanent employment. So if you have the option of taking time out it may be worth considering picking up a new skill, anything from typing and computer skills to acupuncture. Many courses are available either on a short block basis, or by attending weekends and evenings. It's worth investigating.

28

For:
- you rarely forget a skill once you've learned it, and computer skills can come in handy in any job these days
- it's something else to add to your CV
- a short course and the added skill may make it easier for you to find temporary employment before higher education
- if you can't find a job, a course can help you structure your time and develop an interest

Against:
- not all courses will be free
- many courses are privately run, so you will need to seek them out
- they may only fill part of your time, so you'll need to consider what to do the rest of the time
- not all will lead to nationally recognized qualifications, so care is needed with selection
- if you do find you qualify for financial assistance on such a course, it could affect your entitlement to grants later, so *beware* and always check with the local education authority first

6. Mixing it and filling the gaps

While planning ahead is excellent, most people find that their plans alter as time goes on. Even the most well-planned year may contain odd surprises and about-turns. The main thing is to plan your first move and remember to plan subsequent moves as far in advance as possible, preferably *before* they become necessary. You could start out by taking a six month au pair job in France, then travel for a few months around Europe, run out of money and have to return to the UK to take a waitressing job in the summer until college starts. That's fine, but if you run out of money or have your wallet stolen you need to have some contingency plans worked out. The list of possibilities which could contribute to your 'mixture' is endless, and entirely depends on your sense of adventure, your resourcefulness, your initial research and subsequent planning.

For:
- if you take a year out before higher education you may actually have more like 15 or 16 months to play with – that's a lot of time to fill
- taking time out before committing yourself to higher education, or before entering a career after you have finished your diploma or degree course, could be the only time in your life that you allow yourself the freedom to move around and be selective, ie, before you 'settle down', get a mortgage, get on the promotion ladder etc., so the more you pack in the better

Against:
- if you don't plan and make decisions about how you are going to spend your time you risk drifting and ending up doing nothing in particular
- you could lose sight of your reasons for taking time out
- your CV could look a little empty for that year if you just 'messed about'

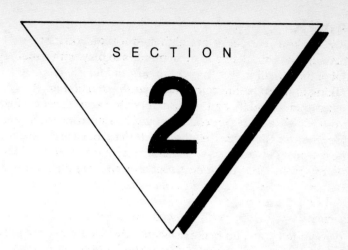

SECTION

2

Consumer views

You are not the only person who will have views about taking time out. Most of us want (or need!) to take into account what other people may think:
- *parents (what about financial and emotional support?)*
- *employers?*
- *admissions tutors?*
- *the point about time out is that you come back . . .*

Family focus

Parents and family may not be able to stop you doing something you've decided to do, but you can't always shake off their influence. They can be very helpful with your choices, but on the other hand their opinions can be the opposite of yours. Either way you are likely to have to take their views into account, and it's probably better to get them on your side from kick-off.

Before looking at how you might persuade them to your point of view, here's a look at how one parent reacted to her daughter Helen's decision to up sticks and go to France and Spain for a year after her A-levels:

Mum – Well she wants to be a translator or an interpreter, and she's aiming for a degree in French. We did look at some of the prospectuses and it seemed that one or two of the colleges preferred them to have done a year abroad first. She was all for it! First of all she came up with the au pair idea, but I was a bit uneasy about that. If she could get into a good home then fair enough, but you're never sure. And in any case she's not equipped for it, she's no good at housework, and when it comes to babies she wouldn't know which end was which! But then she came up with the idea of getting an assistant post in a school for six months in France and six months in Spain, and I felt that was preferable.

The whole thing seemed to start a couple of years ago when the school asked if we would take exchange students for a few weeks. We did, and then she was asked back. It was quite a

shock as before that she wouldn't even go into town on her
own, and suddenly there she was flying off in the wide blue
yonder, changing planes in Zürich and going across the Swiss
border into France. It did her the world of good!

I'm not really worried about her idea of going off for a year.
Not *now* anyway. If she had still been as she was a couple of
years ago, rather quiet and retiring, then I think I would have
been worried to death. But with this more outgoing attitude I
think it will work well. I think things should improve greatly,
especially as she'll have to fend for herself and she's never had
to do anything around the house here before. Apart from giving
her the opportunity of seeing a bit of the country that she wants
to work in later on, I think it'll do her good in other ways, as
she's going to have to stand on her own two feet. She is fairly
sensible, but there are things that will crop up that she'll find
difficult to cope with. But I doubt if she'll give up if things get
hard as she's very determined. And if she rings up sobbing her
heart out I shall just tell her to get stuck in and make the best of
it. I shan't be offering her an easy way out!

Helen – I first started thinking about taking a year out when my
Spanish teacher suggested that spending a year abroad would
be good for my languages. This was about the end of the first
year of A-levels. At that time I had no idea what I wanted to do,
but I got hold of a book that had some contacts in it for becoming
an English assistant in schools in France and Spain.

Before I came up with ideas, Mum and Dad were worried I
might just waste a year, but they got more keen when I got a
clearer idea of what to do. To being with I was quite keen on
becoming an au pair, but my Mum wasn't keen on that as she
said it would be like being a slave! So I've changed my ideas
since and they aren't putting any restrictions on my plans now.

It wasn't too difficult to think of good reasons to persuade
them. I said that it would improve my languages a lot and help
me to gain confidence, and that I'd also get first-hand
knowledge of the country and the people. And I'd also get more
used to people, and would get work experience too. But they
haven't really been against it. If I hadn't had any clear ideas I
think they wouldn't have liked it at all. They certainly wouldn't

have liked it if I was just going to mess about. They wanted me to have definite plans. My Mum agrees it will be good work experience, and that's what a lot of firms are wanting. And I think I would have just got fed up with the course if I had gone straight to university without a break.

There will probably be quite a few problems to tackle at first, with the new language and the way things are done in different countries, and I suppose it could be quite lonely. If I rang home and said I didn't like it I think they would probably encourage me to keep at it and not give up. They wouldn't want me coming straight back home at the first sign of difficulties. I think they worry a bit about me being on my own in a different country, a long way from home, but they just tell me to keep in touch. I hope to sort out things like accommodation before I go and I intend to save up so I've a bit of money which should help too.

I think the main thing I shall get out of it is work experience, but also going before I start my course should give me a head start with the languages and will help me to know more about the countries and how things work abroad. I don't think I'd take a year off if I weren't doing languages. Doing it this way means I'm doing it for a definite purpose.

College concerns

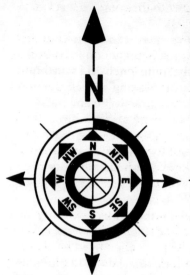

Obviously course tutors recruiting linguists will welcome time out, but what about other areas of study? Peter went along to sound out John Pickles, Industrial Training Tutor at the University of Huddersfield, who is responsible for obtaining one-year-long industrial placements for students on mechanical and production engineering sandwich courses.

Peter – I kicked off by asking him if he thought that only the industrial year out was of value, or did he think that other ways of taking a year out could be beneficial. He explained that it really depended on what students did with their year out. "It has to be constructive", he said.

Apparently the university gets lots of different types of people applying; about two-thirds are 18 year-olds who apply in the conventional way, straight from school. But the other third don't fit into that category, and they may have done anything beforehand. They might have missed the boat first time round. Or done an apprenticeship, got to a junior management position at the age of 23 and then decided to work up to professional level by taking a degree course. It seems that some give up very good jobs to go to university and their attitudes are different; they make very good students.

Some students have spent a year travelling before starting their degree. John isn't particularly put off by this, but fewer and fewer fit into this category. Others have been unemployed for some time before they apply. Just occasionally a student drops out of the course but rejoins after a year. An engineer who failed his first year exams took a year off, got a job as a barman on a liner, then went back to retake the first year. He became one of the department's star pupils!

I then asked John if it was common for students to take a year out after completing their degree or higher diploma course. He could only think of one who had gone on to do voluntary work for a charity in Nepal. The idea of taking a break after the completion of a degree course is very attractive to engineers because of the intensity of the course work and industrial experience, often extending through the vacations. And a spell of travelling can bring advantages; for example international companies may welcome the student who has experience of living abroad, and who can thrive in another culture. But taking time out after a degree is less likely to be a realistic option when jobs are more difficult to get. "I advise the students to enter jobs as soon as they can in this market", he said. "Employers are not so interested in last year's graduates."

John went on to talk about the industrial year. The students work as a member of the company's staff on real projects, although in training. They are supervised by members of the university staff and company trainers, and draw up a comprehensive log book of their activities. As well as their engineering work, they examine the business objectives, structure and career progression within the company. And prepare their plans for a final year project.

Experience with an employer at this stage holds quite a few advantages for students. They gain structured work training, which counts towards Chartered Engineer status, and they can play a useful work role. Often the experience brings out different qualities and skills; having to communicate ideas to other members of a team, for example, or analyze practical problems. Tutors observe a more positive attitude to study on their return and a strong commitment to the final year project.

And what do the students think? Very few do not enjoy the industrial year. They are enthusiastic about getting working experience before committing themselves to a more permanent contract with an employer. And gaining references that may help them to find work after their degree. For some students there is the added benefit of learning and using a second language in a work setting. John has been arranging language training and placements in France, Belgium, Germany, Czechoslovakia and Holland. "We're looking at Malaysia and Barbados, too", he said.

I asked John how students on sandwich courses fared when looking for work, compared with other students. "Quite simply, they get the jobs", he said.

While interviewing John Pickles, Peter also found that there had been some research at the University into the advantages of taking a year out as part of a sandwich course, whether for engineering or for arts courses. The findings highlight his comments:

Advantages of a year out on a sandwich course

- the year out does not just result in technical experience, but is linked to personal gains
- communication skills improve
- students can see the relevance of what they are being taught in the final year of the course – having seen its application in industry – and this enables them to gain much more from their lectures
- many found it hard at first, taking about three to four months to acquire the specialist knowledge available within their chosen company to a level which enabled them to make a full contribution
- most found it a good time during which to make mistakes, which they felt they could not afford in their later career
- those who were unsure what to do after graduation felt that it helped them to decide
- the year gave them a chance to try something out without commitment
- it was a good way of finding out what was wrong if their original choice of career turned out to be at fault.

Kate, a student at a sixth form college asks
John Brown, Postgraduate Admissions
Tutor, Department of Social Policy and
Social Work at the University of York what
he thinks about taking time out.

Kate – What are your views about taking a year off?
John – Taking a year out gives students a year away from the environment they've been used to and this can be a good idea, although it can also be unsettling. If you come straight from school you're thrown into a completely new environment which I think people cope with much better if they've had a year out.

The number of mature students we are recruiting has increased dramatically, and this can create difficulties with people straight from school. The differences can be considerable – those who have taken a year out can integrate better with the changing complexion of student experience. Also, people are now coming into a first degree from a variety of alternatives – not just GCSE/A-levels. Many have vocational qualifications and have had work experience, and this changes expectations.

Also, on a practical note, times are hard – if you can get a job before university this may give you some resources that can provide a degree of ballast for student loans.

For graduates, especially if they are not certain what they want to do, a period of time out can be invaluable. If at the end of this they still feel they want to do a postgraduate course with us, it is a sign of real commitment. Whether we are recruiting for undergraduate or postgraduate courses, we want a clear impression that candidates know why they want to do it, that they haven't just drifted into it. We also want to know that they haven't just drifted into the year out – we are looking for people who have looked ahead and planned the next five years; have taken time out as a conscious choice and not just by default.

Kate – Are there any particular kinds of experience or activity that you might favour?
John – I think generally any activity is going to be useful. The worst thing is inactivity, where you sit at home watching television till it goes off. Whether you spend a year abroad, working as a volunteer, or working in a shop, it's important to do something which broadens your network and contacts. It can eventually help people to get that extra degree of self-confidence which helps them to contribute to debates. A year out can help especially for those coming into social science courses. Anything that broadens experience in terms of different situations can help contribute to degree studies.

Kate – Before we leave that, John, given that your students are studying areas concerned with society and the community in various ways, do you have any preference for people to do community work or voluntary social work?
John – I don't think it makes much difference what the experience is, as long as what the person does is well thought out and structured.

Kate – Are there any negatives?
John – Individuals do become anxious about writing essays after taking time out of education. Often that anxiety is unfounded. The skills that people pick up when they are at school don't disappear so quickly. But it is important for them to keep abreast in terms of reading up on current affairs while they are out of education. They should do anything to keep the brain ticking over, rather than just drifting.

Kate – As an admissions tutor would you say then that you are unequivocably in favour of students taking a year off?

John – Yes, though I think I should say that I am tending to look at deferring entry from the point of view of the person actually considering it, rather than from the point of view of a university which may be trying to recruit sufficient students to keep its course viable. All further and higher education colleges are now looking for older students to fill the available places; and that although in principle admissions tutors might feel it is a good idea to defer, some may at the same time ask students if they have considered the advantages of coming straight to college after A-levels.

Kate – That's very interesting – are you saying that admissions tutors may put pressure on applicants not to defer for a year because they want commitment before they change their minds?

John – I think 'pressure' is too strong a word. In the past you would have found admissions tutors pointing out the real advantages of taking a year out, but you may find now that they put the points over less enthusiastically than they did. They may start to mention the difficulties of picking up study again, though I don't think there would be real pressure.

Kate – Finally John, I know that you are also responsible for recruiting postgraduates. If you are advising someone who had to choose between taking a year out between school and college, or taking time out after graduating and before employment or further study, which would you recommend?

John – I think I would definitely recommend taking a year out before a degree. There are benefits from having a year out before college, in that students settle down and contribute positively to their course afterwards. Certainly from our experience at York, students who don't come straight from school often eventually get better classes of degree (first class honours, or a 2:1) than those who come from school.

Also, I think if you take a year out after graduating, employers may well wonder why you decided to take time out at this particular time. If you have done a degree which equips you with various professional skills, employers may feel that you have lost the edge, lost the momentum you have built up if you take time out. Personally I think there is possibly more to lose by deferring entry into professional training and employment after a degree than there is at the beginning.

I also think there can be pressures put on you from within the department in which you are studying, to go out and get a job as soon as possible. Departments can be evaluated by how successful they are in actually getting their graduates into jobs. It's the sort of thing that all universities make great play of when people are invited to come and see why they should read a particular degree; information is available showing what kind of employment people are in six months after graduation. So you may think it's a good idea to take a year out, but you may find everyone trying to encourage you to get into employment. We are keen on this because it reflects on our degree courses when we are trying to market them to prospective applicants.

Kate – That's refreshingly honest John, because what you are really saying is that applicants should bear in mind that departments have their own interests to serve, and may not give absolutely objective advice on taking time out.
John – Yes, I think it's particularly important that all applicants think through the situation from their own perspective and are clear about what they can contribute to a course, and what they want to get from it – and when! Also, we are moving towards a time when people have a sense of personal development throughout their working lives, and much greater flexibility in when a degree can be taken. It could be that some people will defer entry to university until ten or 20 years after leaving school.

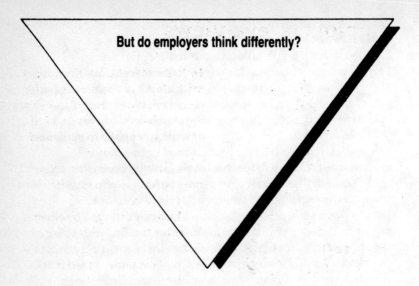

But do employers think differently?

Employers' eye-views

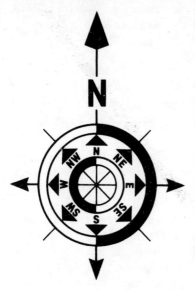

To find out just what employers might think about people taking a year out, either before or after higher education, or even whilst at work, we spoke to personnel officers of two major international recruiters, who employ both A-level applicants and graduates.

Adrienne Irving, Personnel Manager for the Leeds office of Grant Thornton, an international firm of business advisers, and Erica Town, Group Graduate Recruitment Manager, Nestlé UK Ltd, a multi-national food company, share their views and experience:

Q – In general, how do you view applications from A-level students and graduates who have taken a year off?

Adrienne – We would regard this very positively, providing an applicant has used the time to develop themselves. What is important is what they have made of the opportunity. If it has built their personality, taught self sufficiency, the ability to budget, given maturity, this is an asset. If these qualities do not emerge, then the fact that they have missed this opportunity to develop would probably count against them.

Erica – Yes, it's a question of how people explain it to you; if you gain from it a clear picture that somebody has changed and developed, are able to do things differently afterwards, I would say it is a positive thing. The real negative is, if, after a year, people reflect back and still say "I wasn't sure what I wanted to do" and don't tell us what they have learnt from that time out. There need to be clear objectives, both about what they want to do and why they are doing it. It doesn't matter too much what people do – if someone did a lot of temporary jobs and could talk about the personal development they had gained from them, were able to analyze the experience including the negatives, we would see this as broadly relevant.

Q – Do you have any views about whether it is better to take time off after A-levels or after a degree?

Adrienne – For students entering employment directly after A-levels, a year off which is well spent can have an even greater impact than for a graduate, who has had a chance to develop some of the qualities we are seeking during their time at university. Sometimes, an A-level student will be leaving home for the first time when they go to our Training Centre, and we need to spend a lot of time building up their confidence. A-level entrants are important to our company – for every graduate we employ we bring in three or four A-level trainees, in whom we are still looking for interpersonal skills in developing relationships, managing staff, influencing people, managing time and recognizing qualities in other people. A well-spent year out can mature an A-level applicant, but they need to be able to explain what the benefits were, what they gained from the experience.

Erica – I agree that post A-level, it's a particularly good idea providing there are clear objectives on what the year out is there for. Somebody who says "I want to travel" and earns enough to finance it in the first six months is likely to have a clear view of what they are getting from their time out and why they are doing it.

On the negative side, we sometimes get the impression that people have taken a year out because they haven't really decided what they want to do, or because they are being forced down a path they don't really want to take – perhaps into a degree they don't really want to do – and are hoping it will give them breathing space. In general, however, if people take a year out after A-levels, they will go to university better equipped and are able to get more out of it. It is a good transition to independent life.

Adrienne – If a graduate applies to us, we consider the total person presenting themselves to us; how they acquired the personal qualities and experience we are seeking is less important as long as they can demonstrate it. We would certainly find it strange if someone gained good experience between A-level and university and failed to build on it during vacations or took advantage of other opportunities offered in their university lives. It certainly doesn't work against an applicant that they are joining us a year later, we are putting a lot of responsibility on them, so it doesn't matter if they are a year older (although we do look very closely at applicants over 25). Gone are the days when things are handed to us – school, training, employment. An applicant needs to be able to have something to offer; they need to work hard on their application; they have to work hard at interview, even harder at our Assessment Centre – then take on seven plus years of hard accountancy training. Some of these qualities are manifest in the experience people gained on the year out – but it would certainly count against them if they had a year out and wasted it.

Erica – Another important point is that A-level students and graduates need to understand the cycles of recruitment. We recruit A-level candidates during the summer, three to four months before they start work, but graduates are usually recruited six months before starting work so it's important to be around at the right time. Sometimes it can turn into *two* years off – and then it is really important that candidates can talk about what they have gained, what they have learnt and how relevant this is to the job they are applying for.

Q – Is there anything you don't want to hear from applicants who have taken a year out?

Erica – I always ask "what were the high points and low points?" and often hear "everything was great!". This doesn't really tell me anything – it can't possibly all have been marvellous. This can demonstrate a lack of realism or that someone hasn't really thought about the building blocks of the experience. A good candidate will tell you how they encountered some major problem and how they coped with it. This is an extremely strong indication to us of how they would cope with new challenges of work.

Adrienne – I wouldn't be impressed by an application form which simply said "one year out – travelling". I would be looking for signs that it had been planned and had direction and had equipped them and benefited them.

Q – How do you feel about sandwich placements as a form of 'year out' for students?

Adrienne – The firm favours this – we can find this a good recruitment aid, as it gives the chance to 'vet' future potential staff. We take students with all sorts of degrees, not just Accountancy. We would be more impressed, however, if the 'sandwich' year out were planned and an integrated part of the degree course, rather than a student just organizing something for themselves to have a break.

Erica – We are generally in favour of sandwich placements, but problems can arise when the *quality* of the placement leaves a lot to be desired – for example, if a student is given a year of clerical work which does not give them the chance to explore their own potential. We always ask "could they have done something about it? Did they try?". If they tried, they get marks for initiative even if it didn't achieve anything. We want people who will challenge the status quo. Did they take the opportunity to learn a language, develop computing skills – how did they turn a disaster to their advantage? It is possible to learn from a poor quality situation.

We are also moving to recruiting students from sandwich courses in shortage technical and engineering areas, where we have more difficulty recruiting candidates of good quality. If we find good students, we may offer them a job at the end and consider sponsorship for their final year.

Q – Do you have a company policy about taking a period of extended leave from work?

Erica – Not really, although we do a fair amount of secondment across the business as part of management development, both for A-level entrants and graduates. We also arrange exchanges with other organizations like the Ministry of Agriculture, Fisheries and Food. Secondments might be overseas – generally in Europe at the early stages, but this may lead to opportunities much further afield.

Adrienne – We don't have a firm-wide policy as such, but we do offer work-based secondments. All our graduate trainees (although not yet our A-level trainees) have to have a secondment, usually for a year – which might be in the UK but can be in America, Canada, Germany, France, Belgium etc.. We also have secondments outside the firm – to the European Commission, for example, or the DTI (Department of Trade and Industry).

Most secondments are organized by the firm as part of an individual's career development, but it is possible for an individual member of staff to negotiate a secondment themselves, with our help – although there is no guarantee of a job on return in this case. Someone has just returned from a secondment she negotiated in Nassau in the Bahamas; she had to accept, however, when she went that there may be no guarantee of a job back in the UK afterwards.

Q – What are you looking for when you interview applicants?

Erica – We are looking for very specific skills. Our training programme demands a high level of adaptability, and successful candidates will move through different functions and working environments where they will need the capacity to absorb information quickly and to make decisions based on their judgements. Because of this, we are seeking evidence that someone can offer an analytical mind and logical approach to problem-solving, is persuasive and able to communicate ideas clearly on paper and verbally; is organized, methodical, pragmatic, independent and self-motivated; able to work under pressure and take responsibility for their actions. Where we hear that time out has offered the opportunity to demonstrate and develop some of these qualities, we are very interested.

Adrienne – In our selection processes, we have identified certain areas of personal attainment and personal qualities, and it is possible to use experience gained in the year off to demonstrate that you can offer these. They include how you plan and organize; your influencing style; how you relate to others; your achievements; how you deal with pressure; your breadth of view and approach to problem-solving; and your views on business.

Applicants who can draw on experiences gained in the year off to demonstrate examples of why they believe they possess these attributes are definitely at an advantage.

Pulling it all together

Feeling swamped by all this? You knew that people would have different reactions, but . . . It might help to bear in mind some of the following issues when putting your case to parents, college tutors and potential employers:

Parents' views

Parents probably have a lot of influence on what you do between A-levels and higher education; even after graduation the chances are that they will take an interest in your plans, and may have views. They may be a help, or they may be a hindrance, but *they* are the people who probably know *you* best, and their views are worth taking into account.

So, what are your parents likely to consider when you broach the subject of taking time out?

- **your safety and happiness – do you know where you will live, how you will earn money; will you be on your own or accompanied?**
- **your ability to cope with looking after yourself, especially if you are going to be away from home for the first time**
- **whether you are mature enough, and whether the experience may help you to grow up and fend for yourself**
- **whether your choice for time out is likely to benefit either your study or your future career**
- **how future employers may look at your time out**
- **whether you are doing something 'relevant' to your later choice of course or career**
- **whether you have made sensible plans, or are you likely to waste your time**
- **are you able to finance yourself, will you be earning or have you enough money to travel?**

University tutors

University tutors are hoping to fill their courses when they interview you. So what are they going to be considering?:

- **they tend to accept that a large number of their students will not have applied for courses in the conventional way at 18, in order to start straight after leaving school**
- **they see some benefits in having more mature students on their courses**
- **in some subjects, they may be concerned that you will have forgotten essential basic knowledge on which they want to build**
- **some may be slightly worried that older students may find it hard to settle down to studying again**
- **they like students who have had some previous relevant experience**
- **they seem unworried by students who have taken time out to travel**
- **those that run sandwich courses believe that their students mature in many ways while out on their industrial year**
- **performance indicators in the new 'Academic Assessment' which universities have to undergo take account of departmental success in graduate employment . . . they are likely to advise students leaving higher education to consider securing a job, before going off around the world, although this advice may not be easy to follow**

Employers

While parents have their opinions, and tutors hold the key to whether or not you attend their courses, it is employers who will ultimately be paying your salary. What they see on a CV influences whether they bother to interview you or not. So, how important are those spaces between courses of education, or between finishing education and taking up work?

What do employers take into account?:

- **they may accept time out, but will expect you to be able to explain what you gained from the experience in terms of personal development and maturity**
- **they prefer students to have spent their time doing something which gives them practical experience to add to their academic training**
- **they are likely to be suspicious of inadequately explained gaps on a CV**
- **they may think you were unable to get a job if you didn't go straight into one on leaving a course**
- **they are not keen on people who appear to have been drifting**
- **they are there to make a profit or provide a service and are usually more preoccupied with these ends than with your individual happiness**
- **they tend to like students who have spent time out on work-related activities, either before or after a course, or as part of a sandwich course . . . sandwich courses are looked on very favourably as the placement ties in with the academic work**
- **if you leave a job to take time out they are unlikely to penalize you if you reapply later on – provided they saw you as a good employee in the first place**
- **their main interest is in how good you are likely to be or have been at the work they require from you**

Painless persuasion – Getting them on your side

So you still want to take time out? How are
you going to persuade your family to
wave you off enthusiastically, and
your future college or employer
to welcome you back with
open arms on your
return?

Everybody will prefer you to produce INFORMED plans which
will give you RELEVANT experience for your long term aims. It
is easiest when you know exactly which course or job you are
coming back to and can show that your time out can give you
more to offer. Hardest is when you haven't a clue about your
long-term plans and are hoping that inspiration will descend
during your time out!

You are likely to be more convincing if you think through,
carefully, where you are with your life and career plans
generally:

Which describes your present position best?   *Tick*

A. I am certain I know what course/job I want after my time out.   ☐

B. I think I know the broad general area of work or study I am aiming for.   ☐

C. I haven't a clue what I want to do in the long term; perhaps time out will help me to decide.   ☐

If you ticked box A above:

Have you applied for your course yet? If not, why not get the interviews out of the way now and see if you can defer entry?

Course(s) applied for: _____

_____

Date(s) _____

Outcome _____

What do you think your tutor's reaction may be to you taking time out? If you don't know, write and ask for an informal discussion to check over views and get advice on the best form of experience to acquire.

Tutor's name _____

Wrote for informal discussion on _____

Visited tutor on _____

Summary of reaction/advice _____

_____

Why do you think your time out might help you to gain more from this course?

> I will gain more from this course because _____
>
> _____

If you are coming back to a job, is there any chance of deferring a firm offer of employment? Have you tried?

> The job I hope to do is _____
>
> _____
>
> Companies I am interested in _____
>
> _____
>
> Letter of enquiry on _____
>
> Summary of reply _____
>
> _____
>
> Applied for job on _____

If this isn't possible, do you know how this particular occupation recruits? Are there lots of vacancies throughout the year, or will you have to be careful not to miss a closing date? If you don't know this, check it out with your careers service, or with the appropriate company/professional body.

Jobs in _____

are usually filled by (describe main methods of time of recruitment)

_____

I got this information from _____

_____

How will you explain how your time off will enhance what you can offer as an employee?

I will have more to offer to a company after a year off because _____

_____

_____

_____

_____

_____

_____

_____

You may have to be prepared for more than one 'year off'. If you can't enter employment immediately after your return, how will you spend your time?

Jobs I can look for _____

_____

Courses I can take _____

_____

Voluntary work I might do _____

_____

If you ticked box B above:

What experience or contacts will your time out give you that may help you to decide that your tentative interests are right for you?

Activity _____

_____

Experience gained _____

_____

Possible contacts _____

_____

In what ways will your time out help you to learn about yourself?

Three things about me I hope to check out during my year off

1. _____

2. _____

3. _____

Look carefully at the career areas that you are exploring and think about how you will decide it's for you. What might be helpful to be clearer about in terms of your interests, skills and values?

Interests – Things I enjoy doing _____

_____

_____

Skills – Things I feel I am good at _____

_____

_____

Values – What is important to me _____

_____

_____

For how long can you afford to defer a decision? If you are not sure, check closing dates for application to courses, or the usual job recruitment procedures, either direct or through your careers office.

Course/Job _____

Usual closing date if any _____

How does this fit in with my time out? _____

_____

Do I need to change my plans to take account of this? _____

_____

If you ticked box C above:

Especially if you don't know your long term plans, it's important to be very clear and well organized in planning your time out. List all the things you have thought of doing:

1. _____

2. _____

3. _____

4. _____

5. _____

Look at each in turn. What do you think you will gain from this?
(It's OK to have fun, but what else might you gain in addition?)

Plan   Gains

1. _____   _____

2. _____   _____

3. _____   _____

4. _____   _____

5. _____   _____

Are there any specific issues that you can use the time to learn
more about (eg how you feel about HOW you want to work with
people; can you cope with forms and figures; how good are you
at thinking on your feet; are there any particular skills you might
develop . . .?)

Things about myself I can discover which can help my long-term plan

_____

_____

_____

_____

_____

_____

Draw up a timetable for your time out:

_____

_____

_____

_____

_____

_____

_____

_____

Draw up a timetable for your return:

The week I come home I will _____

_____

By the time I have been home a month I will have _____

_____

If nothing has happened by Christmas I intend to _____

_____

Make a list of people you will contact to talk through your experiences with, and think about how this can help move your plans on:

Name	Job/Position	How can they help?

If you ticked A, B or C above:

Think about your immediate plans. How much money will you need?

Initial expenses (clothes, passport, insurance, etc.) _____

_____

Travel _____

Food _____

Anything else _____

How will you obtain this? (and if borrowing, how/when will you pay it back?)

I will need about £ _____

I can obtain this by _____

_____

If I borrow, I will pay it back _____

I will earn the money for that by _____

_____

_____

Who do you need to contact to make travel arrangements?

Name   Job

By when?

Date _____

What arrangements have you made for accommodation, if
appropriate?

What contingency plans have you made if things go wrong? (If
in doubt, consult section 3.)

What might go wrong for me? _____

_____

How will I cope? _____

_____

Identify all the reference books which may be helpful. (See
section 4.)

Title	Author	Publisher

Finally? Look back through 'PULLING IT ALL TOGETHER' –
page 49. Are there any possible concerns left which you guess
your parents/employers/tutors may feel?

Parents: _____

_____

Employer: _____

_____

University: _____

_____

How would you address them? (Be specific about how and
why.)

**If you have managed to find answers to filling THREE
QUARTERS of the boxes, then you are likely to be very
convincing in persuading people that you are doing the right
thing – and reassuring yourself too!**

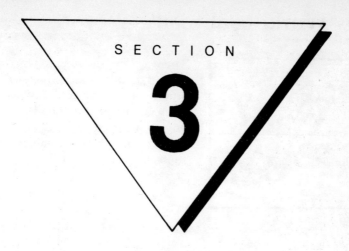

SECTION

3

The best laid plans . . .

You have probably already heard travellers' tales and tall stories from people who have taken time out. Is there anything to be learned from their experiences? Read on . . .

1. Working abroad

There are various ways of working abroad, in full-time permanent employment, on a voluntary basis or by taking casual holiday employment. Rose decided to travel on a fairly well-established route around Australia before she started her degree course.

Dear Sue,

I'm finally getting organized with the trip to Australia. Having applied for a deferred place at university, I was beginning to feel rather nervous – Have I burnt my boats? Was this wise? Why not go to university this year, like everyone else? But I met someone at a party last week who'd just got back from Oz – he'd had a really good time, and gave me lots of useful advice. So I'm really excited now.

And I've found someone else who is going out at the same time – do you remember Jane, the tennis star? She's got a year to fill before she starts her course too, so we'll travel together and see how it works out.

I'm hoping to work for at least some of the time – have to really, because I can't save that much before we go! We need a Working Holiday Visa, which allows us to travel for up to 13 months, but to work at the same time – as long as we don't work for the same employer for more than three months. Sounds ideal! I'm still getting conflicting messages about the job situation, though. Some people are saying there won't be any work because of the recession, high unemployment levels etc.. But others say that if you're prepared to go where the jobs are, and if you arrive with good references and CV at the ready, there is still plenty of casual work about. Difficult to know what to expect.

I've been saving like crazy, just in case. The fare is going to cost about £7–800 at the time we want to fly, and I need to have some £2000 put by as a guarantee (a condition of the visa). So I'm banking all my Saturday earnings – and it looks as if I'll be working in the pub for the summer holidays, waitressing. We hope to go in October, which gives me extra time to save – and apparently there is more chance of work when we get there, because the Australian students won't have started their long summer holiday. With any luck we'll be able to take some time off over Christmas – and just go to the beach!

We're starting in Sydney, and after that who knows? I'm going to buy an Explorer bus pass before I go – so that I have an itinerary worked out. But it's up to me when I travel – so I can see what work there is, what the places are like – and who I meet, of course. I want to get to see my aunt in Cairns, but there are so many other things to do. The Australian tourist information is mind-blowing.

Meanwhile, people at school seem to think I'm crazy. Maybe it seems too frivolous an adventure when everyone is so worried about jobs, competing in the market etc. And I will be a very long way from home if anything goes wrong. At least my parents are a bit happier about it now – the more I find out, the less they seem to worry. For instance I can join a contact point when I get to Sydney, so that my mail can be held in one place. The people there will take phone messages, and give advice on travel, work and so on. And my parents know they can get hold of me.

Have I convinced you that you should come out too? I know you were wondering about trying to take a year out. I can tell you about the permits etc. if you want. I guess it depends on money, as usual.

I'll be in touch again after the exams. Best of luck with the Economics.

Rose

Cairns, Queensland

Dear Sue

Sorry I haven't written, but there's been so much happening since we arrived.

Where to begin? We flew into Sydney as planned in mid-October. We had booked our first few nights in the hostel before leaving, with the flight. That was really useful, just being able to collapse for a few days; the long-haul flight was exhausting. And the people in the hostel were just so helpful; they picked us up from the airport, advised us on travel, arranged trips etc.. And there was a noticeboard for jobs, too, so we got some work shortly after we arrived. I did a very basic clerical job for a few weeks with a bus company, and later some leafleting for a dry cleaning company – handing out promotional material to commuters every morning as they came out of the station!

After six weeks we headed north. Jane and I soon decided to go our separate ways. There are definite advantages to travelling on your own – you can go where and when you want. At the same time you are constantly meeting up with people in the hostels, so you're never lonely – quite the reverse! After Sydney I headed for Brisbane, and ended up working in a resort called Surfers Paradise, this time as a waitress. When I wasn't working I tried out all kinds of things – from windsurfing to bungee jumps. And went with friends to the mountains – lots of waterfalls, wildlife and a rainforest climate. Four of us got a flat together in the end.

At the moment I'm in Cairns with my relatives. It's super to see them, but I'll be glad to move on again. I'm joining some friends on an outback hike starting at Alice Springs – camping, walking, and spectacular scenery, at Ayers Rock and King's Canyon. And maybe the opportunity to learn how to throw boomerangs, and see some aboriginal art. Sounds great doesn't it? But I'll be out of money after that, so it's back down south to Adelaide for some fruit-picking. Then a short stop in Melbourne – and home.

This trip really is the best thing I could have done. I feel much more positive about the course next year, I have got school out of my hair, and it has been really good fun – working, organizing my life, travelling, meeting completely different people. What I hadn't expected is just how vast the country is, and the distances I am getting used to covering. Just getting to Cairns from Surfers Paradise took the coach the best part of a day and night!

I haven't really had any major problems so far, apart from having my camera stolen. The surprising thing is how welcome you are here as a traveller. Back-packers make up part of a huge travel business – and they are very well catered for. Can you imagine being able to pick up free travel guides, and find comfortable hostel accommodation (with swimming pool), as soon as you landed in Britain? The hostels are clean and cheap, about $8–10 a night, and then you can cut costs more by travelling with people who have a car, chipping in with petrol costs.

And getting a job has not been as difficult as I expected – maybe because I told everyone I met from day one that I was looking for work. I soon learned not to expect anything too grand – waitressing and bar work are the norm. At the start I signed on with lots of agencies for typing work, but most of the better jobs go to people with experience. The main thing is that I've managed to pick up enough work to stay solvent.

I shall be very sad when this year has come to an end. I am planning how to come back when I have graduated – to explore Western Australia. I'll know next time to buy an 'open jaw' ticket, so I can arrive and leave from different places, and allow more time to travel back through Asia. Maybe I'll include some really exotic stopovers; Bangkok, Bali, Singapore. . . . Are you sure I can't persuade you to come out next time?

Hope your course goes well. See you again in July.

Rose

2. 'The world in a year' – travel and holidays

Jackie waited until she had finished her degree studies before taking a year out to 'travel the world'. Taking a Year Off spoke to her about her experiences.

Taking a Year Off – When did you decide you were going to take a year out?
Jackie – I'd always wanted to do it and after finishing my degree seemed the optimum time, before settling down to a job. I also thought it might help me clarify what I wanted to do.

Taking a Year Off – Why did you decide to travel?
Jackie – I'd always been interested in travel. I'd done quite a bit in Europe, mainly holidays, and I had always been interested in different cultures and societies. I didn't see it as a useful thing for either college or work – to be honest it was really enjoyment and self-interest that motivated me!

Taking a Year Off – How did you decide where you were going to go?

Jackie – I probably decided on the basis of very little knowledge. I had a hazy picture in my mind of South East Asia and I was very attracted to that, with its Buddhist culture, but I realized as soon as I was travelling that what I had made my decisions on was very spurious. I had stereotyped opinions about places. I did do a lot of preparation – reading travel books from the library – but many of those were out-of-date and didn't give a good impression of what the countries are like now.

I went along to a travel agent and found out about the variety of routes you could take by plane and found one of the cheapest that incorporated South East Asia. It went to Sri Lanka, Bangkok, Singapore, Djakarta, Sydney, New Zealand, Tahiti and Los Angeles. Then it was up to me to arrange the ticket from Los Angeles home to the UK. However, within that, I changed my mind quite a bit once I had set out.

Taking a Year Off – What other planning did you do?

Jackie – I did some general research. I wrote to all the embassies finding details about visa requirements. Then I did all the administrative bits like getting the visas, getting vaccinations, booking flights and all those practical details. Most of the information I got was from embassies and talking to people who had done it.

Taking a Year Off – Did you go on your own?

Jackie – Yes. At the time I horrified myself by the idea of going on my own and spent a great deal of effort trying to persuade people to go with me. Now I'd say that that was the biggest mistake I made, in the sense that I think I got most out of it being on my own. I did in fact advertise in the *Youth Hostel News* for someone to travel with. A lot of magazines do this. I got about 70 replies, and chose someone local. We got on surprisingly well, but after a month and a half decided that it would probably be best if we travelled on our own from then on. I think I got far more out of travelling on my own than I would have done in company – you meet a lot more interesting people

when you are on your own than you do when you have the
security of someone with you.

Taking a Year Off – How closely did you stick to your plans?
Jackie – I think I stayed fairly close to them mostly because I had
to be back by a certain date as I'd arranged a postgraduate
course for when I returned. Having said that, things changed
quite a bit while I was out. For example I hadn't intended to go
to India or Nepal, and it was only on the advice of people on the
road telling me that I should visit Nepal that I went, and of
course I realized that they were right – it is a fascinating place.
So I changed my itinerary quite a bit and the length of time I
stayed in places. I had totally underestimated how long you
need in a country to even begin to see part of it. So I would
emphasize that, that the world in a year is just not possible!

Taking a Year Off – How did your family react to your plans?
Jackie – It varied. My mother thought I was mad, she couldn't
see why on earth I should want to do it – she's never been
abroad in her life! They were all quite worried for me, especially
when I went alone, but I think they were also quite proud. I did
my best to allay their fears by keeping in regular contact, with a
letter at least once a week.

Taking a Year Off – What were the biggest problems you encountered?

Jackie – Day-to-day living could be a hassle. You have to be prepared for everything to happen a lot slower, and not to see as much as you'd like. The slightest thing takes a lot of effort, just getting a visa or booking a railway ticket – you can't believe the bureaucracy, the inefficiency sometimes. You make plans, then a train is two days late and you have to argue with people about why you've missed your plane, and change all the bookings. So things don't happen as they do in Britain. In addition you have to adjust to all the other associated things, like the heat and the strange food. One of the biggest problems I encountered was getting ill. It's almost standard that anyone who travels at that sort of level, certainly in Asia or other developing countries, is going to get ill at some time, usually with diarrhoea, so you tend to accept it as part of the package. I was laid up with dysentery for a month in Nepal. I was in bed for ten days and was very weak and could hardly eat or drink. It took me about two-and-a-half weeks to recover. That was my worst time, but even then you aren't just neglected in a hotel room, everyone knows you are there even if you're travelling alone. I took loads of anti-diarrhoea tablets with me, but nothing coped with it. But as soon as you see the local doctor, they give you one tablet and you're fixed up! So it isn't worth worrying too much, although it is sensible to take advice and not drink the water or drinks with ice-cubes etc..

Taking a Year Off – Did you anticipate problems before you set out?

Jackie – Oh yes, lots! But most never materialized. I thought no-one would speak English, but the only place I had some difficulty was in Thailand where very few people spoke English; but again they were very friendly. Everywhere else, everyone was desperate to learn English and as soon as you arrived anywhere they would come up and talk to you. So that meant you couldn't learn any of their language even if you wanted to! The other things that had worried me were personal harrassment, having my money stolen, being a woman alone, getting raped or attacked. I wouldn't say you shouldn't think about them as I think the fact that I thought about them made me safer. I did meet a lot of people who had had travellers cheques and cameras stolen – many were sitting in hotels, waiting for American Express to reimburse them. But mostly if you were sensible and kept your ears and eyes open and knew where these sorts of things happened you could generally get by safely.

I think in retrospect there were probably aspects of the trip that I missed out on because there were things I would have done if I'd been a man. Generally, especially in Asia, I had no trouble. It was only when I hit Australia and America that I encountered any problems in that respect. I think having a healthy suspicion of people's motives kept me safe.

Taking a Year Off – What sort of things did you take with you?
Jackie – I had thought about taking toilet rolls, as I thought you might not get them in India! But of course you can get toilet rolls even in the smallest villages. I should have taken the minimum of clothing, but I took as much as I could fit into my rucksack and then groaned for a year! Hard-wearing stuff is sensible. A sleeping sheet is useful as you are often sleeping in unsavoury conditions and it's nice to think you have something of yours that is washed. The other thing I found invaluable was a padlock, because if you are sleeping out on your own you have to padlock your valuables to you, or to a wall, or to the bed and it's useful to lock people out of your room, so a variety of them is useful. But if I had to go with one thing it would be a guidebook. I know some people disapprove of the idea of going with a guidebook because it defines everything you should see, but I think I would have found it more difficult without one. I used the Lonely Planet guides. They do a shoestring guide to virtually every country, but there are others too, and more up-market ones. Everyone who was travelling in Asia seemed to be using the Lonely Planet ones. They give you a map of every major town, and places to stay for your first night, and that's comforting. The bad thing is that absolutely everyone who's travelling ends up at the same three hotels in each town, but then it's quite nice to meet someone you met a few weeks ago.

Taking a Year Off – What about the practicalities, like passport, visas, money etc?
Jackie – Getting visas was always a hassle. I got some in the UK before I went. That's difficult of course if there's a limited time on them and you're not sure how long you will be in any one place. I usually got them from the country I was in before setting off. And regulations can change quite quickly, even while you are travelling. Virtually everyone took travellers cheques, which is a nuisance because you pay interest cashing them all the time. But there isn't an easy way of dealing with money and if you lose travellers cheques you can get them back very easily within a couple of days, so it's most sensible.

Taking a Year Off – What advice would you give to other people thinking of doing the same thing?
Jackie – I'd say not to be put off, worried or frightened by the idea. It's much easier than you think. There are a million and a half people doing it and you think you are going to be the only one out there – a pioneer in India with your backpack! Then at the first hotel you meet just hundreds of people all doing the same, and they all speak English! What I would say is that it's going to be the most rewarding thing you are going to do. And if you don't like it you can always catch the next flight home!

Another way to see something of the world is by voluntary work abroad; see Anila's story on page 81, Finlay's story on page 85 and Daniel's story on page 104.

3. Voluntary work at home

Community Service Volunteer

Becky took a year off between A-levels and her degree, in order to work with the Community Service Volunteers. It was an experience which she is glad she had at that time, as can be seen in a conversation she had with a friend who was also thinking of doing CSV.

?

Bev – Why did you take a year out?
Becky – My Dad was one influence. You know he's a teacher and was very keen on the idea of my taking a year out from education. I also wanted to earn some money and get some experience of working, either in the community or in some way helping and caring for people. At that time it was what I thought I might like to do, and I wanted to test it out.

Bev – What was it about CSV that made you choose that kind of work?
Becky – My sister had done CSV so I knew about it from her and I wanted to do something which brought me into close contact with the public. I thought it offered the choice to do something I really wanted. All their material implied they would match you to an appropriate project, which would try and give you something that was a challenge.

Bev – Where did you go and what sort of work did you get to do?
Becky – To Stockport, for seven months. I was based in a social services office with a youth and community worker, and my main project was to organize a summer play scheme for a really run-down estate that was demolished soon afterwards. Because I was in social services I got involved in setting up a mums and toddlers group as well, and visiting an old people's home on a regular basis and helping at a luncheon club for old people. I

served dinners and chatted with the old folk. I also got involved in lots of other little things, like clubs and outings on a less regular basis, mainly with handicapped old people and children.

The work on the playscheme was mainly administrative, but I also had to canvass the people on the estate and find out what their opinions were and whether they would get involved. I did a lot of this on my own, and sometimes it was quite frightening for an 18 year-old. The estate itself wasn't very welcoming, although the people were OK. I had to find premises and apply for funding for the project and try and find out where we could get volunteers from. I had to talk to people who worked with the estate, like social workers and educational social workers, to get an impression of the types of people we were dealing with, and the types of kids they were. I also went through a lot of files to check age ranges we were looking at.

Bev – What about the hours, were they regular?
Becky – Yes, but I did a lot of evening work as well, not at youth clubs, but at clubs for the physically handicapped and mentally handicapped.

Bev – What was it like living there, did you get a flat or bedsit, and did you get to meet anyone else?
Becky – I was lucky in that I shared a council flat with two other CSV volunteers – it was on the 11th floor of a block! And obviously we did our own catering.

Bev – Being voluntary work you don't get paid do you, so how do you manage to live?
Becky – It's better than you imagine as the flat, heating and electricity were paid for. You also get a food allowance and pocket money. (It's about £21.50 per week now, 1993.) It's not a lot of money, but we found it quite adequate to get by on.

Bev – You mentioned having flatmates, but what was the general social life like?

Becky – I lived with the two other volunteers and the local co-ordinator arranged a couple of meetings with some other volunteers. And there were another two volunteers in Stockport too, so we arranged to meet them. We all became quite good buddies! We also mixed quite well with the social workers and other people in the flats, as well as people in other voluntary organizations. It was great!

Bev – So do you think it's worth doing. I mean, what do you think you got out of it?

Becky – I'm not really sure what I expected, but it was time well spent. I met a lot of people from all sorts of different backgrounds, I saw a different side of life, and I had to fend for myself. Without wanting to sound corny, I think I did grow up during that time. I became very aware of how lucky I was, through seeing a side of life I hadn't seen before. I like to think that feeling has lasted. I asked my mother if she thought I had changed and she replied that I seemed a lot less selfish and was thinking more about other people and less about myself than previously. In addition to that, I did get experience of working. The work experience was useful – I had to be more disciplined, get to work on time, stay till five o'clock and had to get on with people of all ages. And it helped me realize that I did want to eventually get a job that involved being with people, working with the public.

Bev – So what are your lasting memories of it?

Becky – I made a couple of enduring friendships. I was always busy doing lots of different things which I enjoyed, meeting lots of people and I felt like I was doing something constructive and practical to help people. I was organizing things to help them enjoy themselves a bit more, and I got people together like with the mums and toddlers group.

Bev – Was there anything that was difficult or that you didn't like?
Becky – I think I found it difficult to organize my own work, even though I had some help. And it's sometimes difficult to get to know new people. I also worried that I wouldn't want to go back to college and that it would be hard getting back into studying. But it wasn't a major problem, though it took a few weeks to readjust.

Bev – What's your opinion then, should I do it?
Becky – Yes, it's something that I would definitely recommend to other people, both from the point of view of taking a year out and doing the voluntary work. It's too easy to get caught up in the tide before A-levels and you tend to do things your friends are doing. You concentrate on your studies and put in applications for universities and you don't seem to take time out to think. However, I applied for a degree a month after I'd started on CSV and I still made the wrong choice by doing history! The year out also seems even better in retrospect than it did at the time. You appreciate having had a break before taking a degree course. I haven't met anyone who regretted taking the break.

Bev – But what about employers, when you've been for job interviews, what do they think about your time out?
Becky – I've found that it's been a bonus, an extra experience to talk about. When I applied for jobs after university it was very useful to have something other than vacation work to show as evidence of organizational ability, evidence you had got grit and had got the nerve to get up and do something different. Very few in my year had that.

4. Voluntary work abroad

Voluntary Service Overseas

VSO offer people who already have qualifications, the opportunity of two years' overseas service. The majority (40%) of these are teachers, while others are in agriculture, nursing and other occupations. Anila qualified as a nurse and midwife, and her experiences of a two-year stint in Nigeria provide an insight into volunteer work abroad. 'Taking a Year Off' checked out her experiences . . .

Taking a Year Off – Why did you decide on VSO?
Anila – I'd always wanted to do voluntary work abroad, but I never really thought I would, so I decided to apply to VSO and see what happened. I applied in May, knew by June where I was going and went in September – so it was all quite quick. Before I went there was a ten-day skills course in Bristol, for volunteers in all different work areas, the idea being to prepare you for your trip. You do commit yourself for two years, but there isn't a contract to hold you to it. I had an individual interview, and a panel interview, where they ask you about your qualifications and experience, and try to assess how you would cope in odd situations miles from anywhere, without electricity and so on. Then I was accepted.

Taking a Year Off – How did you feel when you knew you were going?
Anila – I didn't believe it. I didn't feel that I was really going until I got there! I was placed in Nigeria, and once I got there I enjoyed it so much I thought about extending my stay. I only came home because of problems in Nigeria, and for a family wedding.

Taking a Year Off – What happened when you arrived?
Anila – I wondered what I had let myself in for, but that feeling didn't last long. I soon got busy. I was never tempted to go

home. The people there really help you to settle, they were warm and welcoming and very anxious to keep you! I was never left to get lonely. But it did take about nine months to settle and to really know what was needed, that's why a long stay is necessary if you are to be productive. It was completely different from how I imagined it though. I thought the conditions would be a lot better than they were, and that communications would be better. The nearest phone was 50 kilometres away. I think you need a bit of maturity to cope with it all.

After an orientation week in Kano, where you meet all the other volunteers in Nigeria, you are taken out to the projects and introduced to everyone there, including the project head. That took a couple of weeks. Then I got into the job. Basically I was left to get on with it. I had to work with another midwife, and we were part of a team, with other aides who were not fully qualified and two doctors. I spent some time observing while I worked out what the needs were. Then I started working in nursing and midwifery and re-organizing the ante-natal clinics. I worked in the hospital, which was 45 kilometres from the nearest town and I also went to a clinic along a bush road twice a week.

The work was different from how I had imagined. I was surprised at the number of people who weren't trained and they didn't have the equipment that was necessary. It was very hard to adapt to these conditions – you have to learn to be content with very little success in persuading people how to do things.

Taking a Year Off – What did the local people make of you?
Anila – They seemed really excited to meet me and wanted to see what I looked like and what I could offer them. I think it was because I was a stranger and they seemed to have more faith in foreign medicine. The doctors I worked with were very glad of the help and were very supportive. They were keen on anything I wanted to start up like a babies clinic twice a month, where we had 80–100 babies through between 7.30 and 3.00. Women would trek anything from 10–15 kilometres to come once word got around.

Taking a Year Off – Were you paid and where did you live?
Anila – Yes, you get paid the local rates. It was enough to live on. I had a very basic house in the hospital compound. It had two rooms and a toilet and shower outside – a bit like permanent camping. The family next door had the same, but there were ten of them! So it was adequate enough, but then I'm not really a fussy person. The shower and toilet didn't always work. Sometimes there wasn't any water. We had wells, but they needed the electric pump, and the generator was constantly breaking down, which affected the hospital. We would then get a tanker in, but that had a limited supply. The worst thing was the lack of water – you can get by with little food, but without water things get difficult.

Taking a Year Off – What did you enjoy most?
Anila – I think when you go you have to be very open-minded and not have high expectations. I enjoyed all my time there. But probably one of the best things was teaching people how to make soya milk. Nigeria has no fresh cow's milk and dried milk is too expensive. So I was teaching them to make milk at health education classes. Then someone came up to me in the market and asked me how to make it, and I knew that I was getting there and felt I had made quite a breakthrough!

Taking a Year Off – What do you feel you gained from your experience?
Anila – It made me a better person all round. I am now very tolerant, more laid-back and patient. I feel I can cope with things better. I think I also became more self-assertive. It certainly made me come out of my shell, I used to only speak when I was spoken to, but because you are on your own you have to be self-assertive.

Taking a Year Off – Did you need to speak a foreign language?
Anila – Not really as English is the national language, but not many people actually speak it. The villagers used their local language, which is Tiv. So I worked through an interpreter, but I picked up the local language in time, so that I could do more health education directly.

Taking a Year Off – How did you spend your spare time?
Anila – On basic things, like getting the water clean, boiling and filtering it, and making my own clothes. I also read a lot of books. And anyway the local people wouldn't leave you alone. When I started feeling comfortable I ventured out to the villages to visit people too.

Taking a Year Off – Were you able to travel?
Anila – I visited other volunteers, teachers and agriculturalists at weekends and also spent four weeks' holiday travelling with a friend, hitching etc..

Taking a Year Off – Was it difficult to return to the UK?
Anila – Yes, in that I felt as if I was back in a plastic world, which wasn't real any more. Everywhere was so busy. Then I had to get used to the constraints of Western living, like the unfriendliness, saying 'good morning' to people and getting a funny look! I got in touch with a local VSO group though, and we have meetings once a month and sometimes give talks, so that is quite supportive.

Taking a Year Off – Would you do it again?
Anila – Yes, in fact I'm very tempted to do it again. I quite like that sort of lifestyle. I felt I was really doing something. I enjoy my work as a health visitor now, it's new and different, but there are restrictions on what you can do. Out there you are more free, you are working on your own initiative and if you feel like starting up new things like parentcraft classes you can do it. I felt when I was there that I was really doing something, and I think that's why a lot of people do go again. In fact some never leave!

To hear another view of VSO, see Daniel's account, page 104.

Raleigh International

Raleigh International is a charity which gives young people the opportunity to carry out demanding environmental and community projects around the world. Volunteers are drawn from all backgrounds and nationalities. They have to be between 17 and 25, to speak basic English, and to be able to swim.

Finlay Dawson applied to Raleigh International during the final year of a Business Studies degree. He takes over the story . . .

Finlay – I'd thought about taking time out and was looking for something constructive to do with my time, perhaps community work. Raleigh was a good option – the work sounded interesting, and I didn't have to have specialist skills. Also the three months' expedition was just about the right time commitment. So I sent off the forms, but didn't really expect that it would happen.

Then I was invited to the selection weekend, which sounded very tough and hard work. You had to sign all these indemnity forms, and were asked if you'd like to raise the amount you were insured for! What had I let myself in for?

Q – And what was the selection weekend like when you got there?

Finlay – It was held on Ilkley Moor, quite local to me. The idea is to push you, to put you in difficult situations, and see how you react. As soon as we arrived we had to empty our carefully packed bags, ditch all our luxuries – then pack up again in two minutes flat. We were put into groups and given a number, and were known by numbers from then on. Two people watch you all the time, so you're pretty nervous. We started to do both practical and mental tests; the first was to build a pontoon bridge over a lake. All the time we were being pushed against the clock, so everybody in the group had to work together; we soon learned that we had to rely on certain people for different skills, and to pool ideas.

Q – Were you told how you were getting on?

Finlay – No, not individually, but the project leaders would comment afterwards on things we could have done better. What was worse was that we weren't fed either; no food at all during the day. Late in the afternoon we had to tramp over the moors, build a bivvy to sleep in, prepare a campfire and finally we had some food to cook. We got to bed late, thinking "right, that's it, a nice rest". But half an hour later we had to get up again to pack our bags and rescue a casualty, all in the dark. It was really tough, very tiring. I came back from the weekend exhausted – but feeling brilliant, full of a sense of achievement.

Q – What happened when you were accepted?

Finlay – I heard soon afterwards that I'd passed the selection tests; this was in March. I could choose which expedition I wanted to go on during the next year or so; providing I could raise some £2950 before I went! I decided to run a raffle, something that I could organize before my finals. The tickets were printed, and letters sent out to companies asking them to donate prizes. After my exams I set out to sell the tickets;

initially to friends and contacts, and then door-to-door. It was all an opportunity to promote Raleigh, to tell people about the work they do in conservation and in the community – in Britain as well as abroad. I really enjoyed it, but wasn't sure until quite near the draw that I had reached the target amount.

Just after Christmas it was time to go. There was a lot of preparation, and the kit cost quite a lot. But Raleigh were very supportive – giving advice on exactly what to get. And I was well briefed about the project in Chile, the work, the conditions. We were to split our time between community and scientific work, and the various adventure activities which are part of the scheme.

Q – And when you set out? What did it feel like?

Finlay – On 13th January we gathered at the airport – full of excitement. The journey took four days in all. When we arrived at the base we were split into groups; then we could set up our tents and relax, really tired. We were all apprehensive, expecting it to be like the weekend; but however tough the next three months was, it was never *that* tough.

A two-day induction course followed. We did first aid, radio operating, river crossings and built bivvies from army-style ponchos – all skills we would use later on. Away from the base we tried abseiling, swam in freezing lakes, and relaxed at a lamb barbeque given by the local farmer. At the end of the induction we learned which group we would join for the next part of the project. None of us felt we really belonged to our group at first, but later on we turned into a really cohesive bunch of people.

Q – Can you tell us about the community work?

Finlay – Our first project was at Exploradores, 22 hours by
fishing boat down river. The task was to build a jetty for local
farmers, to enable them to load cattle on to boats for market.
When we arrived we rigged some tarpaulins to sleep under and
thought we would never settle in – there was nothing there, no
buildings, no people. But after a few days we were quite at
home, and managed during the next ten days to fence the corral
for the cattle.

San Rafael National Park was our next destination. We were
to join a scientific project which was analyzing the rate at which
glaciers were melting. I thought this would be the boring part of
the trip – but the scientists made it very interesting for us. We
dredged the lake, collected measurements, did mussel counts,
and learned about the effects of the glacial waters on marine life.

The project was also rebuilding a path up to the glacier, for
visitors to use. We worked long hours, determined to finish the
path before we left. And we became so involved that it seemed
as if the glacier belonged to us; the sense of achievement was
immense. When we weren't working, we organized evening
activities amongst ourselves, and took a half-day break to go ice
climbing with some experienced leaders. One girl was very
apprehensive, but the group all helped her on; she was thrilled
when she reached the top.

The final project was to finish off a school playground at
Murta, a small mountain village. We built tables and chairs for
the communal village area. This meant that we had to prepare
all the wood ourselves – with no formal joinery skills between
us. We taught English in the evenings. And I learnt some
Spanish on the days we spent working with local farmers. The
locals were so friendly; they fed us, though they had so little
themselves, and lent us their working horses to ride in the
evenings. We were sad to leave.

Q – And the adventure part of the scheme. What was that like?

Finlay – We went to our first adventure project after
Exploradores, to do some sea kayakking. As well as the kayaks

we were given a destination, a map, and some tidal data. We then planned our trip, taking into account the sources of fresh water, and possible bivvy sites on the steep-sided shore. The conditions were quite harsh – we were wet most of the time, had to give up washing our hair, our clothes stayed dirty; but even the most unlikely people adapted.

The wildlife was fantastic – dolphins, parakeets, hummingbirds. But the ration packs were not – sardines, jam, blancmange, milk powder, margarine, crackers. We became quite inventive by the end! It was at this time that we started to gell more as a group. We were starting to support each other, to talk more; and we were also thinking about what we could achieve. While the tasks were always obvious and there were project leaders about, it was up to the group to decide how to do things and how hard we would work. We started to set daily goals for ourselves, and work together more.

Towards the end of our stay we did a tough mountain trek. The challenge was to cover long distances over harsh terrain, carrying all our rations. At the start I was ill, but the others were brilliant, offering to take some of my pack. Then there were other injuries from the partly cleared forest terrain – twisted ankles mostly. We couldn't find the track we needed to reach our rendezvous, and had to hack through the forest with machetes. In the end we turned back to prevent any more injuries.

We were disappointed, even though it had been the right decision. But we had a great welcome when we returned to Murta; and we realized just how much our work had been appreciated.

Q – Were there any bad times?

Finlay – Generally speaking, we stayed fairly cheerful, despite some difficult conditions. But one instance that I remember very clearly was when we were returning to base camp from San Rafael. We were still on rations, and used to fantasize about fresh food. Before we started our journey we sent a radio message to the camp, asking them to book us a cooked meal. But the boat was late, the journey took 38 hours, and finally the captain ran aground. We were all very tired and getting on each others' nerves; and could see the prospect of our meal disappearing. This was a low point for all of us. In the end Raleigh were great; they allowed us an extra day, before we set out for the next project.

Q – And now you're back, what do you think you've gained?

Finlay – I went with some idea of what I wanted out of the experience – self-confidence, management skills perhaps. But I have come back with much more. You learn to look at the way you interact with other people, and how you can contribute to a group. All these things are going to help me – being able to assess my strengths, weaknesses. I've learnt to be tolerant, to listen. And to motivate people – in different ways, according to who I'm dealing with. In a group setting you have to be diplomatic – voicing grievances in an honest fashion, but thinking before you speak.

Q – What are you doing now? And how will you use your experience?

Finlay – I'm now working for the Leeds Permanent, as a management trainee. I had accepted a job with them before I decided on Raleigh but they were very happy for me to go to Chile and join them later. Really all the skills I gained will be useful in my job, especially the experiences of contributing to a group goal, motivating people. And the self-confidence that I gained makes me feel that I won't worry about making presentations and so on.

Everybody got something out of the experience, although we were all looking for different things. You can see people change. Self-development was not one of the things I had expected to come away with, but that may yet be the most valuable result.

For me Raleigh has been the best thing ever; hard work but great fun.

5. The employment option

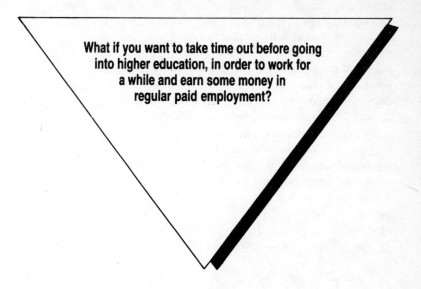

What if you want to take time out before going
into higher education, in order to work for
a while and earn some money in
regular paid employment?

*For many people this could mean taking more than just a year out. The
intention may be to delay going onto a higher education course for one
year, but some people find that they like the job they have taken up, it
may offer the chance of getting higher qualifications by day release, so
you could decide to stay in it for a while longer. After all, the money
comes in handy, and the experience may prove to be as useful as taking a
full-time degree or higher diploma in the long run. So this is the risk
you take if you go into employment – you may end up deciding not to
bother with higher education at all.*

*And this is one of the arguments that people like parents and
teachers are likely to put forward – "If you don't do it now you may not
bother at all". Well if that is the case maybe higher education wasn't for
you in the first place. And many people decide to go into higher
education much later on. It doesn't have to happen just one year after
leaving school or college, you can take a higher education course at any
age. Take the case of Janet who decided she wanted to get off the
treadmill of education at the age of 17 . . .*

Janet – I was never very keen on school, though oddly enough I was quite keen on the idea of a good education. I started taking A-levels, but left half-way through the course. I thought a secretarial course would help me to get a job, so I went to the local college for a year and got the qualifications I needed. I thought at that time that I had finished with academic studies. However, after a year of working as a secretary, it still niggled me that I might have got an A-level in English, so I went to night school for a year and ended up with a grade B. I was so chuffed I decided to take two more by correspondence courses. I ended up with sociology and geography as well. Then I really started seriously thinking about university. It had never seemed possible while I was at school, I didn't think of myself as an academic type at all. But having been out of the system for a while had given me time to think and to decide that as long as it was me pushing myself into studying and not the teachers or my parents then I felt happy. I still had no idea what I wanted to do eventually, but I had enjoyed English so much that I thought it would be a real luxury to be able to study the subject for three years on a full-time degree course.

I thought I would be the only person on the course to be over 20 when I started, but I got a real surprise. I should think about half of the people I got to know in seminars and tutorials were older than the 'normal' 18 or 19, so I soon stopped feeling odd. There were people there who were over 30; one had been in the merchant navy for years, and many had worked in industry, and had decided to make a big change by throwing it all in to come to college.

I also had no idea that I would qualify for a grant as a 'mature' student. By the time I applied I was old enough to be considered as independent from my parents, so a contribution from them was not required.

I found it very enjoyable to go to college after having worked. I think if I had just kept on at school and then gone straight to college that I would never have really thought about what I was doing and why. By the time I got there I had a commitment to studying seriously, though we still had plenty of time off for other things. I had also had time to save some money which came in very handy as it's a bit tight trying to survive on a grant. The other useful thing was that I had done my secretarial studies earlier and I found it very easy to get temporary jobs during the college holidays, and to begin with I also used to take down all my lecture notes in shorthand and type them up neatly – though that didn't last!

Janet found it reasonably easy to find work because of the initial secretarial training that she did – gaining skills that she found useful in many situations later on. But it is possible to go into employment directly after doing A-levels too.

If you are applying for deferred entry to a higher education course, it may be more prudent not to mention this to potential employers; after all, it's always possible you may decide not to go. It is probably best to keep that information to yourself until the final decision has been made. You should always allow yourself the option of changing your mind; you may find that the job offers good prospects and/or the possibility of taking higher qualifications on a part-time basis.

What types of employment are available?

The types of work available depend on the area in which you live, the sort of employment you are prepared to take and the qualifications you already have. You could consider temporary jobs which would probably pay less, but would give you more freedom to finish when you wanted to. Or you could consider permanent jobs. These are more easy to come by if you are prepared to take more general clerical or administrative work, or can find trainee management jobs – in retailing for example. If you are offered a trainee job, which would normally mean you would be a trainee for more than a year, you would have to sort it out with your conscience and decide whether it is fair to take such a job if you are sure you won't want it for more than a year. Even if you have relevant A-levels you would not find it easy to get work in construction or engineering for example, although with science subjects you could apply for laboratory work.

When job opportunities are scarce you may have to take work which is more routine than you would like, for example basic clerical work, or packing – simply to earn some money. Some of these jobs may grow into other things; for example a filing clerk vacancy may lead to a personnel assistant or trainee accountant post, if you apply for other jobs within the organization. But all this takes time, so it is important to consider whether you will get what you want from the kinds of jobs available in a tight employment market.

And what if you can't find any work? The first thing to do is to structure your time, and to fill it constructively. You will find that you can study part-time at your local college of further education, without losing your entitlement to benefit, and without an enormous outlay. Sports and cultural facilities may be cheaper to use, and there may be support groups locally for unemployed people. You can find out about opportunities for voluntary work through your local volunteer centre.

And after six months you may be eligible to join more formal work experience training opportunities under the Government's Training For Work scheme. These can include participating in community work programmes, or training in specific skills, such as computer literacy, upholstery, agriculture, or workshop sessions on finding a job. To qualify you must register for work at your local Jobcentre. All training is decided on a regional basis by your local Training and Enterprise Council (TEC). The TEC will have details of any advanced courses and programmes that are available for graduates too, for example, in exporting or robotics.

6. Short courses at home and abroad

What about a short course (lasting up to one academic year) either after A-levels or H grades and before going into higher education, or alternatively after completing a degree or higher diploma course? Remember that such courses do not always attract mandatory grants, so financial considerations must be taken into account.

Courses may be taken in either the public or the private sector of education, and the range that can be considered is enormous.

Courses between A-levels/H grades and higher education

Why might you choose to do a short course now?

- you could be undecided about higher education
- there may be some particular skills you wish to acquire first, such as typing, computer skills, cooking
- it could be a way of testing the water, seeing whether you like a particular area of study before taking it further.

Why might it be a bad idea?

- if you receive financial assistance by way of a grant, it may affect further grant entitlements later on
- you could be distracted from your chosen course
- it could cost you money, both in fees and to maintain yourself
- a short course could then leave you with some months to fill before you go into higher education
- it may not be full-time, so you need to consider other things to fill your time up or risk getting bored.

What are the possibilities?

There are many different courses, of varying lengths that are now available. These include courses which teach a practical skill, such as computer skills, secretarial, catering or simply cooking, TEFL (teaching English as a foreign language), language study, arts and crafts, childcare, health, fitness and beauty, engineering, agriculture, and so on. Or you could attend college to pick up one or two more academic subjects, which may be required or useful to your later choice of career.

You could opt for a course in a technical college or college of further education, where you may get your fees paid. Or you could choose a course in a private college, where you would be expected to pay your own fees. Private colleges continue to offer courses in subjects which do not appear regularly in the public sector – such as riding instruction, cordon bleu cookery, acupuncture and other alternative medicines, for example.

Your other option would be to take a course by distance learning, either by correspondence course, or through the Open College or Open Tech, which give you the opportunity of a more flexible learning programme. In this way you could combine work with study, which would help with finances.

Courses after a degree/diploma

Why might you choose a short course after completing your higher education?

- you may have had no inclination to learn different skills beforehand
- there may be particular skills which would be an additional help in obtaining employment
- you may have taken a non-vocational course and wish to obtain some vocational skills now

Why might it be a bad idea?

- you may have to pay fees and maintain yourself if you are unable to obtain a grant
- it will delay your entry into employment, which may or may not be a bad idea depending on your circumstances

- you may have to fill time between the end of your degree/ diploma and the start of a short course

What are the possibilities?

The same types of course are available now, as were available *before* higher education. However, graduates may also consider the many year-long courses which are vocationally biased and which are suited to graduates who have taken general degrees and feel they need a vocational qualification before taking up employment. These include the one-year postgraduate teaching diploma, courses in social work, personnel management, tourism, marketing for tourism, arts administration, museum work, advertising administration and many others.

Some postgraduate training opportunities may be available in specialist technical fields through the Training For Work scheme, a Government programme for those unemployed for six months or more. The programmes are administered by the Training and Enterprise Council for your area; details of any schemes will be available through your local Jobcentre.

Courses abroad

Why consider a course abroad?

- it's one way of spending time in another country
- you may be able to spend part of your degree course abroad, in which case it will be arranged for you
- it may give you experience or opportunities for research that you would not have at home

Why not?

- getting finance for a course abroad can be difficult
- applying for courses abroad can be time-consuming and requires a lot of effort to research
- you are stepping into the unknown to some extent, a different educational system

How can it be tackled?

One way of spending time at an educational institution abroad
is to take a course of higher education in this country which
incorporates a term or a year abroad. This is fairly routine for
those studying languages, but is also becoming a possibility for
students of other subjects, including the sciences, engineering
and humanities. Periods of time may be spent with the intention
of learning another language, or could be in another English-
speaking country, where the general degree subject continues to
be studied.

The other way of organizing a course abroad is to do it as an
independent student either between courses, or after
completing a degree or higher diploma. This is by far the harder
option to organize and finance, though it can be done. A lot of
research has to be done, and planning ahead (up to two years in
many cases) is essential. Applications for any available
scholarships should also be made around one year to 18 months
ahead. So, as much advice as possible should be obtained using
the careers advisory services of colleges and the information
sources detailed in Section 4.

7. Time out from study

Taking time out in the middle of a course of higher education is not an easy option, unless it comes as part of a sandwich course. Whilst it is a possibility outside of a sandwich course, it depends very much on your validating body whether they will allow it. Many take a fairly lenient view, but on the whole you will be expected to have very good reasons for wanting to take a break. Time out on compassionate or medical grounds, because of bereavement or other unusual personal circumstances is generally regarded sympathetically. And it is sometimes possible to take time out for educational reasons, particularly if an interesting educational experience or relevant work experience is on offer, which may not occur in the normal way. If this were something course-related, which it could be argued would help with your studies, as can be the case with the Internship programme, then this could persuade many universities, polytechnics or colleges to allow time out. Where this occurs in the middle of a course, remember that you will have to be prepared to rejoin your course with a different group of students.

An increasing number of courses nowadays incorporate a period of time away from college, where you can gain industrial experience, or perhaps work experience abroad. Some have exchange schemes operating with other countries, where the programme of studies continues, but simply in a different context in a college abroad. This can be a valuable experience for any student, not just those studying languages.

Many of these academic exchange schemes are being organized in Europe, as part of the ERASMUS and COMETT schemes. They can offer you the chance to acquire language skills, learn something of the culture of the host country, and broaden your perspective. The study programme or work placement lasts between three months and a year, and becomes an accredited part of your course.

Allison Bennett spent four months studying at the Free University, Amsterdam, as part of her BEd course in Theology.

Allison – "It happened at just the right time for me, in the third year. I was finding full-time study rather stultifying, maybe because I had spent seven years working before I came to college. Ours was the first group of BEd students to go to Amsterdam from the University College of Ripon and York St. John, so I felt something of an ambassador.

The course was accredited as part of my degree, and consisted of theology and education, and a six-week Dutch language course. We also did some teaching practice, and attended the Primary Education Institute, for lectures with Dutch student teachers.

Most of our tuition was in English, in small tutorial groups of English and German students. We had assignments and tasks to do; for example, we compared the Dutch and English education systems, and researched the religious background of Amsterdam. The topics were set before we arrived so we had done some preparation.

The teaching experience was more of a surprise. I was expecting to be in a primary school – but the primary children did not have sufficient English. So the tutor organized two sessions each week teaching religious studies to a class of 15-year-old Dutch students. Imagine my reaction! I had to prepare new lessons and develop different materials. But I learnt a great deal from working with this age range, and having to think how I put the subject over in what was, for the students, a second language. And soon I was able to throw in the occasional phrase in Dutch, which helped.

The tutors were very supportive and made us feel welcome. And we soon got to know a lot of other students, because we lived in a foreign students' residence. The accommodation wasn't brilliant; there were builders working on it, and some weeks the corridors had cement mixers in them. But in time we moved to somewhere better.

The scheme was well funded by ERASMUS; I had an additional £700. Unfortunately the value of the pound dropped just after we arrived, so by the time we left we were short of money. And changing money was expensive; we were not in Holland long enough to open a bank account. But we still managed to include some travel and sightseeing. Getting around in Amsterdam was easy, by tram; and the University lent us some bikes. We felt as if we were on holiday at times.

All in all it was a great opportunity; to experience a completely different way of life, and meet so many other students from different cultures. The school experience has certainly helped with my education studies back in England. It will be a very positive thing to add to my CV too; I had to adapt, to learn how to survive, and develop all the skills that I shall need if I go to a new area to teach. And because we had so much say in what happened to us, I gained in confidence. I know that if I need something I have to ask for it."

The most usual way for a student wanting to combine study with a year out is, however, still a 'sandwich course', where the year out is structured into the course. The major advantage of this arrangement is that the year out is often arranged for you, and where it involves work, it also brings pay with it!

Julian spent his industrial year out (from a sandwich honours degree course in systems engineering), with AEA Technology in Warrington. He was placed in the Department of Electrical Maintenance, and became involved in designing different types of control circuits. He describes his time there . . .

Julian – "I did the two years at university first, and before I went out on the placement I wasn't keen on going at all. But by the end of the second year I had had enough of studying, and I wanted the break. When I got there it wasn't what I had expected, although I eventually settled down and enjoyed it. The first few weeks were quite hard. Basically they didn't give me enough to do at first, I think because I was a student. Then, I explained to the boss that I was getting a bit fed up, and they sorted out some work which gave me more responsibility and helped my confidence. I started in July, but it took until Christmas before I felt I had really settled down. Once you get more responsibility you feel that you belong and you are contributing something.

In the end I felt a bit reluctant to leave, although I did look forward to coming back to university. I had got used to the job, it was relevant to what we are studying. I've been back for three weeks and I'm beginning to realize that I learned a lot, and it's helping with my project here. I feel that I've seen how things have been done, and I've got new ideas as a result. I feel more confident that I can do more now than I could before.

On a general level I feel that I learned to work with people. We had to attend meetings with fairly senior management, who you have to answer to. I think you get more self-confidence in dealing with people. Before the placement you always seem to be looking up to people, but in the job you can be in charge of projects and you might be above other people then. So you have to learn how to be tactful and diplomatic. It was the first time I had really had to work with people. It was also my first experience of a big company, and you realize that you can't be a competent engineer without industrial experience. You think you know it all when you go out on placement, but when you find things aren't done how you expect, then you come down to earth a bit!

On the social side, outside of work, it was rather like being at university. There were a lot of students there, and the company had a hostel where meals were provided. But I eventually shared a house, and the social life was like being at college. It was the work that was different.

Thinking longer term, when I finish my degree I'd like to take some time out. I'm planning to do a PhD before going into industry, so once I get the dates for that I'm hoping to take a few months off to go and visit my brother in Australia. I'll be about 27 by the time I finish my PhD, so this could be my last chance to get out and travel as it won't be so easy to take that amount of time off afterwards – employers might not like it!"

Another way of acquiring 'DIY' time out – in America this time – is through the Internship system. This enables students and other young people to undertake a wide range of paid or voluntary employment in career-orientated placements which can offer valuable specific experience. Opportunities are available in a wide range of cultural, media, social service and administrative organizations from museum work to journalism, law offices to counselling agencies, and up to one third are open to non-US citizens.

One problem – obtaining a visa – can be a difficult and complex process and the type of visa will determine the length and status of the experience. One of the less difficult visa arrangements to negotiate is when the employment experience, paid or unpaid, is an acknowledged and accredited part of a UK higher education course.

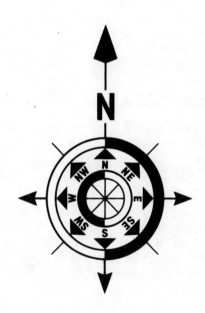

8. Time out after a degree

Daniel read Maths and Philosophy at Balliol, then taught A-level
Maths at a secondary school in Bulawayo, Zimbabwe for two years as a
volunteer for VSO. Since this interview he has joined the Foreign
Office.

Q – Why did you decide to take time out after your degree?

Daniel – I didn't feel ready to go into a full-time job – I don't think that was a particularly conscious thought, but I know that I made no attempt to look at the newspapers or go for the milk round. In fact, I violently reacted against the milk round idea. I didn't want to feel I was penned in or that I had chosen any one path – basically I didn't feel ready to choose anything at all.

Q – In retrospect, was that the right reason?

Daniel – Yes.

Q – Was it as you anticipated?

Daniel – In some ways it was, but I found that I was actually a lot more resourceful than I thought I was. I was terrified – I thought I could not cope with the teaching situation – I thought I would stand in front of a classroom of students and make a complete fool of myself. I was so surprised that I managed to walk out at the end of my first day intact, having actually done quite a good day's work! On the other hand, it took me a lot longer than I imagined to settle down – in fact it took me a whole year. Although I did enjoy my first year I still hadn't created my own life; it was only in my second year that I created my own set of friends rather than being with other ex-patriots and enjoying their company. It took me 14 months before I had a girlfriend and before I was sharing a house with people I wasn't working with – people I had met myself. I also found it much harder than

I imagined to make real friends with locals. The other thing that surprised me was that it was a lot more 'normal' than I expected. It wasn't strange every day. I got used to everything – the heat, the cold, the weather, the people, their habits, their food – it became everyday.

Q – What were the best bits?

Daniel – Discovering that the kids thought I was a great teacher and getting a standing ovation from the sixth form after my first year when I gave them their last lesson before their A-level exam! Eventually making real friends with the local people. Learning a new language and making people laugh because I was so bad at speaking it! Going on the most incredible holidays that I would never have gone on should I have stayed in England. I went to Ethiopia and I also stayed with my girlfriend in Botswana with her family, and helped slaughter and skin a goat which is not the kind of thing that you would do on a package tour! Having to completely change my mental framework.

Q – And what were the worst bits?

Daniel – Leaving! Having to uproot myself again, having uprooted myself the first time in January '91 to go out there, I was now uprooting myself in December of '92 to come back to something I didn't really know at all – recession-hit Britain. I had kept in touch with very few of my friends, having built up my own social circle with which I was perfectly happy back in Zimbabwe. I was very ill in the fourth month of my time there with the worst flu I've ever had – it knocked me out for about four days. I didn't like being ill without family backup. Fortunately there was a woman who was the librarian at the British Council library who was 'mother' to all the VSOs. I took quinine which is the worst experience one could ever wish to undertake (it gives you tinnitus). I thought I was going to die.

Another strange experience was going into the wilderness with a bunch of friends. We'd taken an eight-hour bus journey and then another one-hour journey right into the depths of the bush, and then walked for a day and a half into the mountains and I suddenly felt so far away from home. I'd never been that far away from home – I was an aeroplane trip and a ten-hour bus ride and a one-and-a-half day walk all the way from home – and for about ten minutes I was really scared – but I got over it. And teaching without resources – that was hard!

Q – Are there any ways in which you could have prepared better?

Daniel – This question splits into two. Are there any ways I could have packed my suitcases better – and are there any ways in which I could have better prepared myself both emotionally or physically? I think the answer to the first question is yes, I could easily have packed my bags better. I took books which I had already read which was a big mistake, thinking they would comfort me (they did nothing of the sort – just gathered dust!) and I left my pride and joy, my four-track mini recording studio and I wish I'd taken it with me, because it was my main hobby and on so many occasions I would have loved to dive into it!

The second part of the question – physically, no. I was fit and well . . . that was fine. Emotionally I don't think there is any way of preparing yourself for what you're going to let yourself into. I said goodbye to my friends as best I could and I made sure everybody had my address. I made sure I knew about the country and I did prepare a bit of the language. I knew what climate to expect and what resources – Zimbabwe is middle income. I knew I was going to a city, and I knew that it would be able to provide me with all my basics – soap, sugar, flour, bread, fruit, cheese. You can't really prepare yourself for jumping into a cold swimming pool – if you stand at the side sticking your toe into it then covering yourself with cold water then that will soften the blow a little bit – but it's still going to hurt when you dive in! So I just held my nose and dived in!

Q – How can you make use of the experience now that you are back in the UK?

Daniel – Naturally the experience lends itself to going on to do a

PGCE or some kind of MA or work related to Africa or specifically, Zimbabwe. It's given me a bit of perspective on the way people behave so frantically and manically to some of the situations we face in Britain. The recession for example – there are so many more people in Zimbabwe without jobs.

It's always going to be a place that I can go back and visit. I keep in touch with my friends there – it's a place that is also a home for me. Materially, the options it leaves me for the rest of my life – it's certainly broadened them. I feel I have another reference point now, and I don't have to look at Britain from a British point of view; I can look at it from a Zimbabwean point of view too. I've got depth of field – everything is in stereo – it comes to life, like having two eyes instead of one.

Q – What did you learn about yourself?

Daniel – I think I've discovered that I can't make any fundamental changes to my personality. What I have learnt how to do, is to be more accepting of my own situation, which has then freed me from it.

Q – What has it done for you as a person?

Daniel – I think that now I am much more able to decide what plan of action is going to be appropriate and useful for the task at hand. If, for instance, I have to 'get something done', I would now be in a position to say "well, doing that isn't going to be useful, doing this is – I think it would be a good idea to do that first before I do this".

Q – Can you summarize what skills you feel the experience gave you?

Daniel – Obviously fairly broad organizational skills where I would think the night before what do I have to do tomorrow and prepare for it, and try to envisage all the problems I'd come across, and try to make adequate plans as to how to cope with them should they arise. More importantly, it taught me how to work with people whom I didn't like – how to shut my mind off to various aspects of their character and only focus on the things that they were good for – and to stop treating the workplace as the whole of life. It's not necessarily a place where you make friends, it's a place where you do work, and that's a very different thing. I learnt how to treat people as colleagues and how to get on with them, even if I didn't really like them at all, because I knew I needed things from them. I learnt how to cope with situations that were unforeseen as well – how to improvise on the spot. For instance, nobody told me there was an epileptic girl in my class. Not being scared to take control; learning that you probably do know how to cope with it, whatever it is, and try your best, rather than be scared of it and running away from the situation.

Socially speaking, I learnt how to relate and converse with people with whom I didn't necessarily have anything in common. Before I had been really unable to have a conversation with somebody about something where I knew nothing, but the situation where I was necessitated this because we knew very different things (they knew about Zimbabwean music, I knew about English music). Now that's something that happens in this country too. You might meet somebody whose line of work you've never come into contact with, or somebody who is interested in a composer or an artist or a hobby which you haven't a clue about, and I've learnt how to try and figure out the right questions to ask and get myself interested in it.

Q – So, do you think the past two years have been well spent?

Daniel – Definitely!

9. Time out from work

Ravinder had been employed as a social worker since qualifying two years ago. He's married to Jan and they were paying a mortgage on a house, until they decided to sell the house and travel to India. 'Taking a Year Off' found out more:

Taking a Year Off – Why did you decide to do it?
Ravinder – I think the main reason was that I'd never been to India before and it's where my parents' origins were and you feel a sort of affinity for a place, especially as the rest of my direct family are still there. So I wanted to see the family and I wanted to find out about India as well. We also planned to do some voluntary work while we were there.

Taking a Year Off – Why did you choose this particular time to go?
Ravinder – It wasn't possible when I was younger. I didn't have the money and I felt it important to get straight through the educational system and get a job as early as possible in order to help the family out. I think it's probably easier to take time out when you're younger if you come from a more middle class background, where perhaps you have less feeling of owing something to your family.

Taking a Year Off – What did you do when you got there?
Ravinder – We went to the voluntary project for a few days, but we eventually decided that we could only make a limited contribution there. Meanwhile we were becoming aware that there was so much to see, so we decided to travel for a while and possibly return to the project later. We used Delhi as a base as it's the main place for getting trains and organizing visas, but didn't really plan things, we just played it by ear, using the Lonely Planet guide to India and taking each step as it came.

Taking a Year Off – How did you finance the travelling?
Ravinder – We had both been regraded just prior to leaving, so we had some spare cash. We had also been saving, and we sold the house which gave us money to come back to. But it's cheap to live in India. Most of the expense was in Europe where we stopped off on the way home. We also bought a lot of presents and jewellery.

Taking a Year Off – Did your trip turn out as you expected?
Ravinder – No, in the sense that we didn't stick with the voluntary project. But travelling turned out to be easier than we expected. It's a really easy thing to do, but people *do* worry about it – it's the fear of the unknown, not knowing what to expect. But if you take things as they come it can be relaxing. And I think it's easier if you go accompanied. I think you would have to be a strong person to go it alone.

Taking a Year Off – What did you feel you got out of your time off?
Ravinder – I've been more relaxed than ever before, mainly because the usual pressures were just not there. We only had to worry about where we would be staying for the night and where we would get our next meal. Everything else was our own time, to read, talk to people, play chess etc.. Basically I was able to spend my time as I liked. And I was able to establish contact with family that I hadn't met before. We also saw some amazing scenery on our travels; it makes you realize there is a lot more still to see. I also felt that I gained in confidence, because in this country there are a lot of bad images associated with India, but I felt very good about the people, religion and culture there. I became very positive about what I would now describe as my country. And I also improved my language skills. I would certainly go back again, but maybe not for the same length of time. I think taking a bit of time out is a very healthy thing to do.

Taking a Year Off – Did you take any special precautions before
you went?
Ravinder – You need to take out insurance before you go, and
we had all the jabs and organized malaria tablets and so on. It's
difficult to get good advice on what you need, so it's best to try
your GP and the local health authority, but people get
conflicting advice. In India we felt it wise to be vegetarian and
the only time we got ill was in Greece on our way home! It also
helps to be reasonably assertive, that way you avoid being taken
for a ride.

Taking a Year Off – How difficult was it to get back into
employment on your return?
Ravinder – Not too bad. I approached temping agencies,
explained my situation and was in work again within a month of
being back in the country. I had to be prepared to do anything,
so I took a job as a computer print room operative. Then I got
some youth work as well. After three months a vacancy came up
with my old employer and I got back into the same type of work
I had left.

Taking a Year Off – What was your employer's reaction to your
time out?
Ravinder – At the interview they did ask how I thought the time
out would help my work. I explained that I found out a lot about
the Indian educational system and how it works, and that my
cultural awareness had broadened and my language abilities
improved. I use the language more often with the young people
I meet now.

Taking a Year Off – Was it worth taking the original risks?
Ravinder – Yes. I'd do it again. I feel I have gained by the
experience. I'm a more open person and I feel a sense of
personal achievement. I'm pleased to have taken a risk – I was
frightened at first, by the loss of security, the fear that I might
not be able to cope – were my motives right? What would
happen when we got there? Would we get beaten up? Would

we be able to get jobs when we came back? All of these things worry you, but in the event it took no time to settle. It did help being able to communicate in the language and having some awareness, being Asian, but I think white people feel similarly. Both types seem to fit in, and both types also dislike it, it depends on the individual. Being a mixed couple we were afraid we might be treated as a bit odd, but everyone turned out to be really accepting.

On the whole I think it's too easy to get into a rut. You get married, buy a house, pay the mortgage – it's too easy to get into a pattern of life and behaviour. Our trip broke that and I think that's a good thing.

10. Contingency plans

Jackie travelled; Rose worked abroad; Anila, Finlay and David did voluntary service overseas; Becky did voluntary work in England; Janet took a course and then worked and studied at the same time; Ravinder worked, did voluntary service and then travelled; and Julian took the more traditional route of a sandwich course. They all took different paths, but what they all have in common is that they didn't stick to their original plans. They all had to make adjustments to suit new circumstances. So what happens if your plans go awry, if you run out of money, have nowhere to stay, or have a gap of a few weeks to fill between projects?

What backup do you have?

– your own resourcefulness is your best backup. If you are
  prepared in your plans to take major diversions you will cope.

Working holidays

If you know you already have gaps to fill, then you can plan for them. Working holidays can fill short spaces of a few weeks.

Temporary jobs

If you are not fussy there are many temporary jobs available, especially during the summer months – in catering, agriculture, office work, for example. In winter you could come unstuck as fewer jobs are available for those without relevant skills to offer.

Sign on

If you run out of money and have no job, check your social security entitlements. You may be able to claim enough to keep body and soul together until you sort out a job, or go back on to a grant. It may be possible to attend a part-time course at your local college, while you are receiving benefit, without paying fees.

Go home?

If you are on good terms with your family they may be prepared to bail you out if your plans go wrong.

Offer your services as a volunteer

Many voluntary jobs offer board and lodging as well as some pocket money, and you get experience of real work even if it is as a volunteer. In the UK, you may be able to get placements for a few weeks or months if you don't want to commit more than this.

Try full-time employment

Jobcentres and careers services, as well as private employment agencies have details of vacancies, so check them out. Even unskilled jobs may be worth considering until you decide what your next move is going to be.

Try government schemes

If you are unemployed for some time, find out about the schemes in your area. The names and conditions of the schemes may change, but in general you will have to be unemployed for six months or more to qualify. You may be able to gain work experience, attend short training courses or participate in some form of community action.

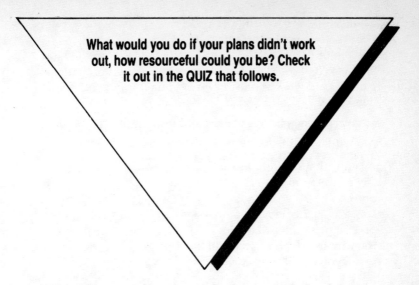

What would you do if your plans didn't work
out, how resourceful could you be? Check
it out in the QUIZ that follows.

11. Can you cope? – Quiz

Check your resourcefulness rating –

Ring the appropriate letter:

**1. You find the driving licence regulations have changed and
you are no longer eligible to drive in the USA. Do you . . .**

a) Go anyway and hope it won't matter?
b) Defer your plans until you can obtain the necessary licence?
c) Check with your employers/American friends about how it
   might affect you to be unable to drive?

**2. You want a year travelling abroad, but haven't any money.
Do you . . .**

a) Pay the deposit for the air fare and hope that your parents
   will turn up trumps when the time comes?

b) Get a temporary job and decide to wait until you have put by £1000 before making arrangements?

c) Book your flight three months hence, take a temporary job and use contacts/reference books to check out the chances of getting paid work at one or two of your stopping off points overseas?

3. You realize that most countries have regulations on entry (visas, work permits, currency restrictions etc.). Do you . . .

a) Assume that students are not affected by this?

b) Get all the forms you can think of and lose heart at the sixth one?

c) Write to all the relevant embassies/consuls describing your precise plans and asking for detailed information about relevant legislation, taking all their information with you when you travel?

4. Looking ahead, the thing that most worries you about your time out is . . .

a) The risk of being bored?

b) Having to cope with strangers in a strange country?

c) Having to come back before you have the chance to do all the things you want to do?

5. When people ask you what you will do when you return from your time out, you say . . .

a) I'll think about that when the time comes?

b) I have a permanent job lined up.

c) I have a course to go to, and I'll review the situation a couple of months before I come back.

6. You know you will be stopping off in a remote part of Borneo where there will be few foreigners. Do you . . .

a) Pack your electronic currency calculator?

b) Empty the local library of everything they stock on the history, geography, culture, cuisine and language of the country?

c) Make contact with someone just returned from Voluntary Service Overseas through their head office and get a list of do's and don'ts and useful contacts?

7. The friend you were planning to travel with has pulled out. Do you . . .

a) Answer an advertisement for an eighth person to share a camper van?

b) Cancel?

c) Go ahead with the original plans by yourself?

8. You are prone to pick up 'collywobbles' in Weston-super-Mare. Before travelling to India, do you . . .

a) Hope your usual tablets will do?

b) Make sure your travelling companion is a qualified doctor?

c) Take medicines you are familiar with, but also plan to use local pharmaceutical resources if disaster strikes?

9. You only have room for one more item in your knapsack. You take . . .

a) Hair spray?

b) Toilet paper?

c) A guide book?

10. You know you don't want to leave this country, but you want adventure, so you . . .

a) Hitch from Land's End to John O'Groats on 50p and what you can earn by juggling?

b) Take a mystery coach tour?

c) Find an organization that offers 'bed, board and spending money' voluntary work for six months anywhere with a group of people you don't already know.

11. You decide to go into higher education after several years of employment, but don't have sufficient A-levels. Do you . . .

a) Write a nice letter to the admissions tutor in the hope that there might be a few unfilled places?

b) Enrol for three A-levels by part-time study?

c) Write to the appropriate department and enquire what arrangements are offered for mature students?

12. You arrange for a period of work experience which you feel is highly relevant to your future course. When you arrive you

find that you will be spending six months doing routine
'casual' work. Do you . . .

a) Pack it in immediately?
b) Do it anyway – at least it earns you some money?
c) Take a list of areas of experience that you hope to acquire to
   your boss, explaining your purposes, try to negotiate some
   space to spread your wings in return for doing a reasonable
   amount of routine work?

**13. You can just afford a three-month short course. You decide
you will take a course in . . .**

a) Sports car racing?
b) Typing?
c) Setting up your own business?

**14. You feel like a break during your degree course, but there
isn't any time out planned into the course. You . . .**

a) Take a year off anyway?
b) Keep your nose to the grindstone?
c) Check the registration regulations to see if there is any
   chance of building a self-arranged 'sandwich' internship into
   the course?

**15. You're 28 years old and decide that a three-year degree
course is what you want to do, but you have to give up a
well-paid job to do it. Do you . . .**

a) Decide to do it anyway and do bar work in the evenings if
   you haven't got enough to live on?
b) Decide to keep on working till you've saved up enough to
   see you through the three years?
c) Check the grant situation with your local authority?

**16. You want to 'do your bit' for society and gain valuable
personal development before you take a permanent job.
You . . .**

a) Spend every night for a week wandering round the roughest
   part of the city, asking people you meet if they need any
   help?
b) Offer to help your mother to deliver a charity newsletter?
c) Contact the local volunteer bureau to find out which

organizations can use your skills and interests or use reference books to get the addresses or reputable national voluntary projects which offer 'bed/board, spending money' opportunities?

17. You're not one of these adventurous types. You just want to get a job locally. Do you . . .

a) Rely on contacts to help you get work?
b) Have a look at what's on offer at the Jobcentre?
c) Go to the local careers office to get some suggestions of what to do and then make speculative approaches to employers?

18. You gain a competitive graduate traineeship with a large, prestigious national company. Then they write to tell you they will have to defer your intake for nine months because of financial stringencies. You . . .

a) Write back and withdraw from the job, saying you don't want to wait to start work.
b) Offer to work for free, or in an unskilled job, in the hope of making a good impression with the company.
c) Accept the deferred entry date and plan 'bed, board and spending money' voluntary work, followed by a couple of months backpacking.

If in doubt about your answers, check through the case studies – it's happened to them! Give yourself three points for each answer (a), one point for each answer (b) and two points for each answer (c).

BETWEEN 42 AND 54 POINTS? – You certainly enjoy living dangerously! Could it be that you are risky rather than resourceful?
BETWEEN 18 AND 29 POINTS – You're a bit cautious perhaps? It is sensible to plan and take precautions, but you may never get started!
BETWEEN 30 AND 41 POINTS? – Chances are that you're going to enjoy your time out and impress family, friends and future employers with your resourcefulness!

GOOD LUCK!

12. Aggie's problem page

Taking time out may be plain sailing for competent yachtsmen, but most people can expect to encounter some problems along the way. So . . . are there ways round them, or do you give in and stick to the straight and narrow?

    'Aggie' sorts out some of the problems 'time outers' have encountered in the past.

Dear Aggie,

I'm in Turkey, having been travelling in Europe for six weeks. I had planned to keep going for three months then come home and get a job. But a couple of days ago I had my money and passport stolen, and I didn't arrange a return ticket back to the UK, so now I'm really stuck and I don't know how I'm going to get home.

Dear Stranded in Turkey,

It certainly would have helped to have organized a return ticket, but even so you might have had that stolen too. As it is I would suggest a visit to the nearest British Consular office. No, they won't give you any money, nor will they loan you any cash. But they will help you get in contact with relatives at home who may be prepared to send some money out to you through one of the banks. They will also sort out your passport problems for you, so try them in case of emergencies.

LOOK AT the checklist for Holidays/Travel on page 134.

Dear Aggie,

I decided to take a year out to decide what degree to do, but I now find that time is passing me by and it's already October and I've not come to any decisions. If I don't apply for university soon I'll have missed out on next year too. I'm so muddled I don't know what to do for the best. Should I just apply for any course to make sure I get in?

Dear Muddled,

Taking a year out is an excellent way of taking stock, but what's the rush? Many people take two or three or even more years out before they choose to go to university. There's nothing magical about taking one year out. If you need longer to decide, then take longer. The main thing to remember is to use your time positively. If you haven't got a job, then get one. Or if you want to travel, start making plans. Taking more time out is fine as long as you don't drift for too long. By the way, you will still be entitled to a grant as a mature student.

CHECK OUT Becky's tale on page 77. She regrets not taking enough time out.

Dear Aggie,

I finish my A-levels in a couple of months and I really want to travel before settling down to college. However, I don't have much money, so I'll have to do it on the cheap, and I'm not keen on going on my own. What do you suggest?

Dear Itchy Feet,

As a student you may get concessionary rail fares (check InterRail), which will allow you to travel cheaply. Why not consider joining the Youth Hostels Association for cheap accommodation en route? You're likely to meet many like-minded travellers in the hostels. If you want a more organized itinerary why not consider a camping trip? There are many arranged by tour operators which can take you to several countries and you are with a group of other travellers.

GO TO the BOOKCASE and browse through the Travel/ Holidays section on page 147. Get hold of the books in the library – they're a good read with plenty of suggestions.

Dear Aggie,

I want to take time out to travel, but my family say I'm nuts. They say a girl shouldn't travel alone as it's too risky. I think I'm pretty resourceful, but how do I convince my parents?

Dear 'Nuts',

I wouldn't say you were entirely nuts, but I can sympathize with your parents. They're bound to worry. However, many have gone before you and survived, perhaps hearing of their experiences may help. Perhaps also spending some time away from home, but still in the UK would help before you embark on your travels. Alternatively you could try and find a companion to go with. You can advertise if you don't know anyone locally.

LOOK AT the section 'Painless Persuasion' on page 52, and READ Jackie's story on page 71.

Dear Aggie,

I'd like to take a year off after I graduate, but I'm not sure how employers will view it when I go for interviews later on. I just feel I've had enough pressure for the time being and I'd like to take some time to decide what I really want to do. I have friends in the United States, so I may go there for a few months and try and get temporary work for a while.

Dear Undergrad,

It's not a bad idea to take time off after getting your degree, but don't delude yourself that this will, in itself, help you to formulate career plans. You need some time to reflect on your interests, skills and values, and take the trouble to check out accurate graduate employment information, which might be difficult if you are abroad.

The really important thing is that you can convince employers that you have spent your time wisely, and that you gained something from it. Most graduate recruiters are looking for qualities like time management, team work, communication skills, budgeting abilities – make sure you give yourself a chance to develop some of these, and learn how to talk about them!

CHECK OUT undergraduates in conversation on page 17. Also look at what employers say on page 50.

Dear Aggie,

I can't stand the thought of being a poverty stricken student for three or four years, so I'd like to work for a year or two before going to college. Can I apply and get a place and then leave it a year or two before taking it up?

Dear Poverty Stricken,

The experience of work can be a bonus, as well as having some extra cash in your pocket. Beware that you might change your mind completely about going to college if you get too used to having plenty of cash. Yes, you can apply for a place now and defer it. Usually you can only defer for one year. Depending on the course you choose, the college tutors may be all for you deferring and working for a while, although some may try to persuade you to come immediately, so think out your arguments in advance of your interview at college.

READ what tutors have to say on page 50. Also consider the sandwich option where you can earn money part way through your course – see page 99.

Dear Aggie,

I worked very hard for my degree and did quite well and now I simply cannot get a job. It seems so unfair – I am willing to do anything and nobody seems interested. I wish now that I hadn't bothered to go to university and just feel like taking off and never coming back. I feel so bored and miserable.

Dear Wasted,

It is a pretty demoralizing experience to find that employers aren't queuing up to use your hard-earned qualifications; but just running away isn't going to help.

Are you really clear about what career will best fit your interests and aptitudes? Have you used your trained mind to research jobs properly? No employer is interested in a graduate who just wants 'any job'. Spend a bit of time using your careers service (or join a graduate job club if one is available) and clarify your long-term plans. Then check out how and when the occupations of your choice recruit. Draw up a list of qualities which will particularly appeal to the kind of employer you're interested in, and THEN plan to take any time available to gain relevant voluntary work experience, a short course which will give you extra relevant skills (in computing or languages, for example) or travelling with a purpose, to build up your confidence and maturity.

Luck is when preparation and opportunity coincide – now's the time for the preparation!

READ what Finlay and Daniel say of their experiences after graduation on pages 85 and 104.

CHECK OUT the Bookcase and see what reference material on page 145 can help with voluntary work or courses.

Dear Aggie,

After I got my degree I decided to take a year off to do some travelling and broaden my experience. Everybody told me this was a good idea – employers are really interested in graduates who have gained some maturity, and got rid of the 'travel bug'. They're wrong! Since I came back to the UK in July, there just haven't been any jobs and I find I've missed out on this year's milk round! I have written literally hundreds of applications – I'm prepared to do absolutely anything – and I feel that I have missed the boat. There are a whole new lot of graduates hitting the employment market this month. What chance do I have?

Dear Unwanted,

People who have told you that employers ARE interested in experience and maturity gained during time out are absolutely RIGHT – but you have to know how to talk about it! No employer is looking for candidates who want 'just anything'; you have to show that you understand what is required of the job you are applying for, what it is about it that appeals to you, and what you have to offer to it. The last bit should be a lot easier having had the chance to extend your life experience – but you need to work hard on analyzing and describing what you gained from the time out.

It also sounds to me as though you haven't taken account of the very different ways different graduate occupations recruit. Only quite a small proportion of graduate vacancies are accessed via the milk round which is normally more appropriate to final-year students and postgraduates who are readily available for campus interviews.

Large national graduate recruiters tend, whether recruiting through the milk round or not, to stick to a fairly regular cycle – vacancies advertised from November through to February; interviews from Christmas to just after Easter. If you are thinking, for example, of personnel or marketing with a large national company who recruit graduates regularly, you are likely to have missed the boat by July. On the other hand, even large graduate recruiters cannot always fill vacancies with applicants of the required calibre and you may be able to pick up some late vacancies, especially in shortage areas, at the graduate summer fairs (your nearest university careers service can tell you when and where they are).

Don't forget, though, that literally thousands – perhaps the majority – of vacancies in small and medium-sized companies are not recruited this way. If you are thinking of something in public relations, tourism, publishing – or any competitive job in comparatively small companies – you need to be prepared to make speculative applications, and look in relevant trade and professional journals throughout the year. One or two graduate possibilities – the Civil Service and the BBC, for example – have only one or two recruitment dates each year.

The message is that – having focussed your career plans – you find out how and when the occupation of your choice recruits. Don't despair, there are still plenty of opportunities, providing you learn when and how to present yourself!

SEE section 'Undergraduates Talking' – Claire has some relevant views, page 17.

13. Is it for me?

Having read about a range of experiences and views, in the end the decision is *yours*. How are you going to decide? It's helpful to think very carefully through what you want from your time out – and WHAT THE ALTERNATIVES MIGHT BE.

Describe in as much detail as possible what your TIME OUT will involve:

My time out will involve _____

_____

_____

_____

_____

_____

_____

_____

_____

_____

Now describe in detail the likely ALTERNATIVE shape of the coming year if you do *NOT* take time out ie, employment, college course. Be as specific as you can about where you would be living, your activities, financial situation, etc..

If I do not take time out I will _____

_____

_____

_____

_____

_____

_____

_____

_____

_____

_____

_____

_____

Personal value rating

How important is the following in your life at the moment? Rate them in order of importance from 1–13:

– having fun
– saving money
– meeting new people
– gaining qualifications
– learning a new skill (specify what . . .)
– gaining confidence in yourself
– feeling secure
– having status
– building on relationships that are already important to you
– taking risks
– being envied
– seeing a clear outcome to your actions
– feeling that you have control over your life
– any other issues important to you (list . . .)

Now look at your top FIVE – the five values that seem most important in your life now (don't worry if you don't feel that these are permanent priorities – it's natural that some will change in the future).

Look back at *each of the options* for next year that you outlined earlier and assess each in the light of your *top five values*, rating them:

1 – If you don't feel the option will give you much of particular value
2 – If it will to some degree
3 – If you feel it will give you a good chance to achieve this particular aim.

For example, if my year off involved working and travelling in Australia, and the alternative was to embark on a degree course, my list would look like this:

Priority	Time out	Alternative
1. Gain qualifications	1	3
2. Meeting new people	3	3
3. Taking risks	3	1
4. Saving money	2	1
5. Feeling that I have control over my life	3	2

The closer to 15 which one of the options reaches, the more likely it will give you some of what you are looking for from your time out. But, it's not just a matter of crunching numbers; the process of thinking this all through is what will help.

Is it worth it?

You should now have been able to decide if time out is for you or not – but at what cost? Whether 'time out' or 'alternative' is your preferred plan for next year, think carefully through the likely scenario and list:

Plan	
Costs	**Benefits (time, money, relationships, risks taken)**

Refer back to PAINLESS PERSUASION on page 52 if your memory needs jogging!

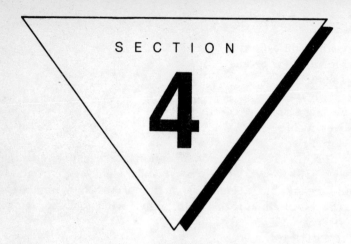

S E C T I O N

4

Taking the plunge . . .

Checklist – things to remember

Work abroad

*Tick those
that need
checking out*

- a return ticket can be useful!

- up-to-date passport

- check visa regulations

- do you need a work permit?

- contact embassies to check any regulations relating to your working in another country

- can you get work organized before you go?

- try and arrange accommodation before you go

- check health regulations, and get the necessary vaccinations

- would a foreign language help? (take a crash course)

- does your driving licence cover you to drive there?

- have you got any contacts you can use, friends of friends, distant relatives etc?

- if you get a permanent job and get removal expenses paid, check what would happen if you want to return home; you may be asked to pay it back

Travel/Holidays

- if you want to get temporary jobs abroad, check any work permit requirements ☐

- have a look at the booklist and get some ideas of work available in the countries you are visiting ☐

- decide whether you want a 'round the world' ticket, or whether to 'go as you please' – you may want to change your itinerary en route ☐

- read up as much as you can on the countries you plan to visit ☐

- contact their embassies and tourist offices in this country and get as much information as you can ☐

- check all health and vaccination requirements; get them done before you go ☐

- decide whether to go alone or seek out a travelling companion ☐

- let your family know where you are going, and arrange ways of keeping in touch, by phone, by letter etc. ☐

- be prepared for your best laid plans to change as you hear of interesting places to add to your itinerary ☐

- accept that other cultures differ, be prepared for both friendliness and hostility, dress appropriately for the country you are in, and respect religious customs too ☐

- take some phrase books if you feel the need and can cope with the weight! ☐

- on the other hand, travel as light as possible, you can pick up cheap clothing as you go ☐

*Tick those
that need
checking out*

– take a travel guide book with you, or a *Cook's Timetable* – decide which is going to get most use ☐

– think about security of valuables, take a body purse or some other means of keeping passport and money safe ☐

– use travellers cheques rather than carry large amounts of cash ☐

– always have contingency plans for getting home if you need to in a hurry ☐

– have faith in your own judgement, while being sensible ☐

– decide how you are going to explain your decision to have time off to travel to employers or college tutors when you get home ☐

– others: add any items of your own

☐

☐

Voluntary work at home

– check out the wide range of voluntary jobs available ☐

– decide whether you wish to stay local or go elsewhere in the UK ☐

– choose the placement either for enjoyment, or for its work experience value ☐

– check out the accommodation that's on offer ☐

– will they be paying you pocket money, as well as board and lodging? ☐

– remember you don't always need experience to do voluntary jobs ☐

– find out whether you'll be working alone or in company, will you be supervised, and if not, can you cope? ☐

– others: add any other items of your own

☐

☐

Voluntary work abroad

– you may be asked for some qualifications and experience before they'll take you ☐

– be prepared to commit yourself to a two-year stint abroad ☐

– be sure you feel mature enough to cope ☐

– expect the worst! Living conditions are often basic, so be flexible and try to accept things as they come ☐

– you're likely to be paid the local rate for the job and get free board and logding ☐

– you probably won't speak the language if you go to
  a Third World country; be prepared to learn at least
  a few words

– approach the experience with as open a mind as
  possible

– expect to take a while to settle down

– also expect to feel unsettled on your return

– check whether you'd be working on your own or
  with other volunteers, you may prefer the
  company

– others: add any other items of your own

Employment

– do you know your National Insurance number?
  You'll need it

– check your tax position with your employer. Make
  sure you pay it – you'll get some back if you go to
  college half-way through a tax year

– decide whether you are doing it for the money, the
  experience or for some other reason; know your
  own motives

- check out the pay, hours and other conditions of service, make sure they suit you ☐

- if you take casual or temporary work remember that you may receive no pay if you take time off for holidays and you are unlikely to have any employment rights ☐

- remember you can still get a grant if you decide to go to college later on ☐

- with some jobs you may be able to take more qualifications while working, or you could take re-sits or extra examinations by night school if you need to ☐

- remember to register at a Jobcentre if you are unemployed ☐

- if you are out of work for a while, research the local training provision. The Jobcentre will have details ☐

- others: add any other items of your own

☐

☐

Short courses

- be prepared to pay fees – if so shop around to find out what different colleges charge ☐

- decide what to do when the course finishes, you may have time on your hands ☐

– if you don't take a local course you may need to find accommodation, check it out first

☐

– try and check on the validating bodies of any course you do, make sure they are bona fide. If in doubt get advice from your local careers office

☐

– if the course is abroad all of this is even more important, and keep a return ticket handy just in case

☐

– others: add any other items of your own

☐

☐

Bookcase

Following is a list of books which can be very useful in your search for something to do with your time out. Even if you decide not to go anywhere exotic, they make for good reading on a dull winter's afternoon! Publishers' addresses are given on page 151.

General

A Year Off . . . A Year On?
CRAC
– a guide to jobs, voluntary service and working holidays during education. Contains many helpful addresses.

A Year Between
Central Bureau
– information on organizations offering placements, projects and further study.

How To Spend a Year Abroad
How To Books
– practical advice on what to do and how to take the decision to go. Includes accounts of people who have taken the year out.

Jobs & Careers Beyond A-levels
CRAC
– covers job possibilities open to A-level students, and further training. Includes profiles of recent A-level students.

Occupations
COIC
– comprehensive careers encyclopaedia, with information on a wide range of career choices, including notes on mature entry.

The Gap Year Book
Cavendish Educational Consultants
– suggestions and advice about filling the gap year, including ways of gaining new skills, volunteer programmes and retake courses.

Time Out
University of Manchester and UMIST Careers Service
– booklet and video which reports on the experiences of over 100 graduates who took time out, and the reactions of employers.

Work abroad

Working Abroad – The Daily Telegraph Guide to Living and Working Overseas
Kogan Page
– practical advice and detailed information on the overseas job market. Details of working and living conditions in 40 countries.

Working in the European Community
CRAC
– guide for graduate recruiters and job seekers, with information on educational and employment practices in each of the 12 member states.

Eurofacts
Careers Europe
– a series of fact sheets about working and studying in European countries. Includes labour market information for individual member states, voluntary work opportunities and titles about specific jobs, such as teaching.

First Steps To Working in the European Community
AGCAS
– a guide for higher education students and graduates who want to work in Europe. Suggests ways of finding work, and includes case studies of British graduates who are working abroad.

Working Overseas
AGCAS
– a guide for graduates seeking work or courses abroad.

Directory of Jobs and Careers Abroad
Vacation Work
– a guide to permanent career opportunities abroad, for those who decide they enjoyed their year out so much they want to stay. Career information for those in the professions. Covers Europe, Australia, New Zealand, USA, Canada and China.

Work Your Way Around the World
Vacation Work
– for the traveller who wishes to work en route. Suggestions of how to find work in advance, or when you're there. Covers grape picking, teaching, au pairing, catering and so on. Also shows you how to 'work a passage', and how to survive when the money runs out. Includes opportunities in Hong Kong, Eastern Europe and Latin America.

Working Holidays
Central Bureau
– see section on Travel/Holidays below.

Directory of Work and Study in Developing Countries
Vacation Work
– covers employment, voluntary work and study opportunities in the Third World. Lists over 400 organizations in over 100 countries. Long and short term opportunities in many countries, including the Caribbean, Latin America, the Middle East, Africa, the Pacific, and the Far East. Looks at engineering, health care, disaster relief, agriculture, teaching, archaeology, construction, medicine and more.

Directory of Summer Jobs Abroad
Vacation Work
– lists over 30,000 opportunities with employers around the world. Covers 45 countries. Jobs for windsurfing instructors, bar staff, bulb packers, chefs, English teachers, farm hands, conservationists and so on. Gives details of jobs, period of work

required and wages, plus full addresses. Also information on work permits, visas and health insurance. Includes some winter jobs, too.

Working Abroad/Working in France/Working in Belgium
Overseas Placing Unit, Employment Service
– a series of brief guides to working in Europe and outside, including information on permits, health and employment. Available from Jobcentres.

Live and Work in France/Spain and Portugal/Italy/Germany/Belgium, the Netherlands and Luxembourg
Vacation Work
– a series of detailed guides. Each volume tells you what to expect when living in one of these countries, and includes information on accommodation, health, education and employment. Major employers and sources of seasonal work are listed.

The Au Pair and Nanny's Guide to Working Abroad
Vacation Work
– lists 200 agencies for nannies, mothers' helps and au pairs. Details of training and experience required, regulations, health and insurance. Covers Europe, North America and Australasia. Includes articles on looking after children, cooking, first aid.

Working in Ski Resorts – Europe
Vacation Work
– information about jobs as ski instructor, chalet girl, teacher, au pair, resort representative and many more, in 40 different resorts. Help with applying via ski tour operators, school party organizers and others.

How To Get A Job in America
How To Books Ltd
– a handbook to help you find short-term or permanent employment. Includes information on pay, conditions and immigration.

How To Get A Job in Australia
How To Books Ltd

How To Get A Job in Europe
How To Books Ltd

Jobs in Japan
Vacation Work
– for English speakers who wish to work as teachers of English
in Japan. Information on over 400 English schools and other
potential employers. Includes advice on coping with Japanese
culture and obtaining visas.

Teaching English in Asia
Vacation Work
– a companion volume to *Jobs in Japan*, listing schools in Korea
and Taiwan, and offering advice on teaching tactics in the
classroom.

Teach Abroad
Central Bureau
– if you want to gain informal teaching experience before
training, or if, as a qualified teacher, you would like to work
abroad. Lists organizations that arrange teacher exchanges,
short- and long-term posts, or voluntary placements.

Teaching English as a Foreign Language and Teaching Abroad
AGCAS
– a guide to work in Britain and abroad, and the training
available.

Courses abroad

Higher Education in the European Community
Kogan Page/Commission of the European Community
– a guide to courses and institutions in each of the member states.

Student Handbook
Council of Europe Press (see 'Careers Europe' p. 151)
– a directory of courses in higher education for 16 countries not members of the European Community, but within the Council of Europe: Austria, Cyprus, Czechoslovakia, and so on.

Eurofacts
Careers Europe
– see 'Work abroad', above.

International Guide to Qualifications in Education
Mansell Publishing Ltd
– looks at educational systems in many countries, covers education at all levels and indicates value of qualifications obtained abroad by evaluating them against standard of equivalent British qualifications.

The Student Handbook
Macmillan Press Ltd
– directory of courses and institutions in 12 countries in the European Community. Includes application procedures, fees, grants, social security, and accommodation. Lists organizations where further information may be obtained and gives tables of subjects.

Directory of Work and Study in Developing Countries
Vacation Work
– for details see earlier section, 'Work abroad'.

Study Abroad
UNESCO, available from HMSO
– details international courses, fees and scholarships.

Awards for Postgraduate Students at Commonwealth Universities
Association of Commonwealth Universities

A Young Person's Guide to Europe
Conservatives in the European Parliament

Study Holidays
Central Bureau
– for details see under 'Travel/Holidays', below.

Voluntary work

Volunteer Work
Central Bureau
– an outline of the opportunities for voluntary service in Britain
and abroad. Includes details of projects, agencies and
organizations involved, and comments from returned
volunteers.

International Directory of Voluntary Work
Vacation Work
– lists opportunities with over 600 voluntary organizations for
both short- and long-term volunteer work, residential and
non-residential. Includes the UK. Organizations require both
skilled and unskilled people.

Volunteering and Overseas Development
Returned Volunteer Action
– a guide to voluntary opportunities abroad, including
exchanges, workcamps, and projects. Work around the world,
including building, farm work, teaching, archaeology etc..

Kibbutz Volunteer
Vacation Work
– all you need to know about working on a kibbutz. Lists over
200 different kibbitzim, describes life and atmosphere to be
expected. Also includes information on other vacation and
short-term work in Israel, from archaeological digs to fruit
picking.

Short courses in the UK

Directory of Further Education
CRAC
– comprehensive directory of courses available in local authority colleges.

Directory of Higher Education
CRAC
– a directory of degree and higher diploma level courses, and professional qualifications. Includes part-time and modular courses.

Travel/Holidays

Educational Holidays
Kogan Page
– guide to residential educational courses and activity holidays throughout Britain. Covers a wide range of courses in 2000 venues. Includes details of some courses abroad.

Working Holidays
Central Bureau
– annually published guide to 99,000 working holidays (both paid and unpaid work) in 70 countries. Offers practical advice on working abroad and details of a wide range of opportunities from crewing a yacht in the Mediterranean to picking pears in Australia.

Directory of Summer Jobs in Britain
Vacation Work
– annually published, lists more than 30,000 vacancies in Britain. Includes sports coaching, farming, child care, archaeological digs, voluntary work and more, and some vacation traineeships providing work experience. Details of wages, conditions, and qualifications are given, together with names and addresses of employers.

Directory of Summer Jobs Abroad
Vacation Work
– annually published, see earlier section on 'Work abroad'.

Work Your Way Around the World
Vacation Work
– see earlier section on 'Work abroad'.

Summer Jobs USA
Vacation Work
– information on 20,000 jobs in the USA. Anything from arts and craft instructors to washers up. Gives wages and details of board and lodging, also visa requirements and other legal requirements for working in America.

Emploi d'Eté en France
Distributed by Vacation Work
– lists opportunities in France, at holiday resorts, summer camps as bar staff or sports instructors and many others. Gives information on requirement for foreign students working in France, with details of wages and hours and any qualifications required. Names and addresses of firms are given.

Study Holidays
Central Bureau
– details of language courses all over Europe, plus practical help on accommodation, travel, grants and scholarships.

The Traveller's Handbook
WEXAS International Ltd
– covers safety and survival, takes a look at food, means of travel and gives information on requirements for visas, vaccinations, insurance, tickets. Designed to travel with you.

Travellers Survival Kit – Europe
Vacation Work
– full of practical advice and information for travellers. Details of the road systems, where to find help and information, border formalities, when shops and banks open, how to use public telephones and transport and more.

(Other titles in this series are available for USA and Canada, Cuba, South America, Central America, Australia and New

Zealand, the Soviet Union and Eastern Europe and the Far
East.)

Budget Travel Australia
Red Sky Publishing & Design
– a guide written by backpackers for backpackers! Includes
detailed information about where to stay, how to get a job, visas
and entry, travel within Australia, and a state-by-state events
guide. Plus some suggestions on making this a round-the-world
tour.

The Traveller's Picture Phrase-Book
Vacation Work
– a novel book, helping you to express yourself in pictures while
away from home and in a country whose language you do not
speak. Covers food, accommodation, travel, emergencies,
shopping, etc.

The Teenager's Vacation Guide to Work, Study and Adventure
Vacation Work
– outlines many opportunities for working and studying during
the school vacations, from picking grapes in France to studying
art in Florence. Also describes adventure and multi-activity
holidays, in Britain and abroad.

Adventure Holidays
Vacation Work
– lists all kinds of sporting and adventure-type holiday
opportunities. Information on accommodation, instruction,
price of holiday etc. Opportunities worldwide.

Hitch Hikers' Manual – Britain
Vacation Work
– gives ideas on techniques, route planning, the law, how to
decide when and when not to accept lifts. Plenty of maps.

Europe – A Manual for Hitch Hikers
Vacation Work
– similar book, covering Europe. Extra information on crossing

the Channel cheaply and some useful vocabulary in ten languages.

International Youth Hostel Handbook
YHA Services
– in two volumes contains addresses and details of hostels in Europe, North Africa, the Middle East, Australasia, America and Asia.

Lonely Planet Guides
– these guides, published by Lonely Planet, detail travel and tourist information for most countries in Asia and for many more in Africa, Australasia and North America. They are stocked by better bookshops. Distributed by Roger Lascelles, 47 York Road, Brentford, Middlesex TW8 0QP.

Time out from study

Study Holidays
Central Bureau
– details of language courses all over Europe, plus courses on art, literature, civilization etc. Practical help on accommodation, travel, grants and scholarships.

Students and Sponsorships
CRAC
– deals with all aspects of course sponsorship. Lists companies which offer sponsorships to students in higher education.

ERASMUS: The UK Guide for Students Entering Higher Education
CRAC
– a guide to institutions offering degree and diploma courses associated with the European Community ERASMUS/Lingua programmes. Includes information on studying in Europe, the European Credit Transfer Scheme and details of schemes.

Internships USA
Peterson's Guides, available from Vacation Work
– details of 38,000 short-term work experience opportunities in
the USA. Includes business, communications, scientific and
other opportunities. Information also on work permit
requirements and how to apply.

Also see prospectuses and alternative prospectuses
– available from colleges and universities.

Addresses of publishers

Following are some addresses of publishers of books in the
above list. Books may normally be obtained through high street
bookshops, but may also be available in your school or college
careers library for reference. Similarly, most of them are
available in public libraries.

Association of Commonwealth Universities, 36 Gordon Square,
London SW1 0PH

AGCAS Central Services Unit, Crawford House, Precinct
Centre, Manchester M13 9 EP

Careers Europe: an organization which co-ordinates and shares
information about work and study opportunities in Europe. Fact
sheets available by subscription or through advisory services
such as your local authority careers service, colleges and
university careers services.

Cavendish Educational Consultants, 22 Hills Road, Cambridge,
CB2 1JP

Central Bureau, Seymour Mews House, Seymour Mews,
London W1H 9PE

COIC – Careers and Occupational Information Centre,
Moorfoot, Sheffield, S1 4PQ

Conservatives in the European Parliament, 2 Queen Anne's
Gate, London SW1H 9AA

CRAC, Hobsons Publishing PL, Bateman Street, Cambridge CB2 1LZ

HMSO, PO Box 276, London SW8 5DT

How To Books Ltd, Plymbridge House, Estover Road, Plymouth, PL6 7PZ

Kogan Page, 120 Pentonville Road, London N1 9BR

Lonely Planet, distributed by Roger Lascelles, 47 York Road, Brentford, Middlesex TW8 0QP

Macmillan Press Ltd, Houndmills, Basingstoke RG21 2XS

Mansell Publishing Ltd, c/o Cassell Plc, Villiers House, 41/47 Strand, London WC2N 5JE

National Youth Agency, 17–23 Albion Street, Leicester LE1 6GD

Red Sky Publishing & Design, 70 Brunswick Street, Stockton-on-Tees, Cleveland TS18 1DW

Returned Volunteer Action, 1 Amwell Street, London EC1R 1UL

Trotman and Company Limited, 12 Hill Rise, Richmond, Surrey TW10 6UA

UMIST, PO Box 88, Sackville Street, Manchester M60 1QD

Vacation Work, 9 Park End Street, Oxford OX1 1HJ

WEXAS International Ltd, 45–49 Brompton Road, Knightsbridge, London SW3 1DE

YHA Services, 14 Southampton Street, London WC2E 7HA

Contacts

Following is a list of just a FEW of the organizations who may provide you with interesting things to do with your time off. There are many such organizations and much longer and more detailed lists can be found in the books referred to in BOOKCASE. We have selected some of the more well-known here:

Acorn Camps (National Trust),
PO Box 12, Westbury, Wiltshire BA13 4NA

British Trust for Conservation Volunteers,
36 St. Mary's Street, Wallingford, Oxfordshire OX10 0EU

BUNAC,
16 Bowling Green Lane, London EC1 0BD

Camp America,
37 Queens Gate, London SW7 5HR

Community Service Volunteers,
237 Pentonville Road, London N1 9NJ

GAP Activity Projects Ltd.,
44 Queen's Road, Reading RG1 4BB

International Voluntary Service,
53 Regent Road, Leicester LE1 6YL

Project 67 Ltd,
10 Hatton Garden, London EC1N 8AH

Raleigh International,
27 Parsons Green Lane, London SW6 4HS

Returned Volunteer Action,
1 Amwell Street, London EC1R 1UL

The Year in Industry,
c/o Brian Tripp, National Director, TYII, Manchester University,
Simon Building, Oxford Road, Manchester M13 9PL

The Volunteer Centre,
29 Lower King's Road, Berkhampstead, Herts HP4 2AE

Voluntary Service Overseas
317 Putney Bridge Road, London SW15 2PN

MORRIS

Jason - Scott

Sallyanne Morris
MARKET
WIGAN

Ex Skem
Ex CHESTER.